PENGUIN BOOKS

THE B.S. FACTOR

Arthur Herzog's *McCarthy for President, The Church Trap,* and *The War-Peace Establishment.* Author of articles for many major publications, Mr. Herzog has also been a magazine editor, a consultant to the Peace Corps, and a political manager and candidate. *The Swarm,* a novel, is his most recently published book.

The
B. S. Factor

The Theory and Technique of Faking It in America

ARTHUR HERZOG

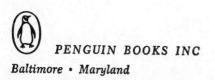

PENGUIN BOOKS INC

Baltimore • Maryland

The author wishes to thank the following for permission to reprint already published material:

The National Information Bureau, 305 East 45th Street, New York, N.Y. 10017, for the "Wise Giving Bulletin," © Spring 1972.

Random House, Inc., for "The World's Biggest Sculptures," in *The Pop-Up Biggest Book* by Albert G. Miller, © 1969. All rights reserved.

Simon and Schuster, for material from *Grapefruit* by Yoko Ono, © 1964, 1970, 1971 by Yoko Ono.

Prof. Marcello Truzzi, for "The Psychiatric Dictionary," by Earl Rubington, in *The Subterranean Sociology Newsletter*, Vol. III, No. 1 (October 1968), pp. 6 and 8.

Penguin Books Inc
7110 Ambassador Road
Baltimore, Maryland 21207, U.S.A.

First published by Simon and Schuster, New York, 1973
Published by Penguin Books Inc, 1974
Reprinted 1974

For BETTY ROLLIN
who is no fake

contents

we have become our own barbarians

—VICTOR PAPANEK

B.S. Factor (bē′ĕs′ făk″ tər), *n. Amer.* : Generic term describing the role of the Empathetic Fallacy* in the national life of Americans, circa 1970. Believed by social scientists to have led directly to the Great Semantic Crash of 1980, when the American language ceased to have denotative meaning and collapsed as a medium of communication. Shortly thereafter, American English was outlawed by the United Nations and Chinese became the official American language.

—WEBSTER'S NEW INTERNATIONAL
DICTIONARY, TENTH EDITION

---

* Empathetic Fallacy: failure of reason and feeling to correspond.

foreword

U PON HEARING about this enterprise, some suggested it might compare with what Hercules confronted at the Augean Stables. B.S., I was told, was so plentiful I ought to be content with publishing an index. I relied heavily on two books I want to mention: *Scepticism*, by Arne Naess (London: Routledge and Kegan Paul; New York: Humanities Press, 1968), a deeply persuasive defense of a mature and misunderstood philosophy, and *Fallacies*, by C. L. Hamblin (London: Methuen and Co., Ltd., 1970), the most complete discussion of the subject that I was able to find.

Generally, I have provided footnotes only for the longer quotations that bear on the commentary, not for most of the numerous examples cited. I was helped in gathering illustrative material by Susan Schoch, Jean Britt, Barbara Butler, and Nancy Riley.

Lucia Gallagher, Kate Russ and Leonard Peters ably typed the manuscript. Robert Brown, Arthur Springer, Betty Rollin, and J. G. Stewart made valuable suggestions, and so did my agent, Candida Donadio. I sent out a questionnaire to a sample of professional people asking them to identify the cant or dishonesty in their work. The response showed that many are alarmed at the nonsense they confront every day. Edith Coulson and I conducted a number of interviews, and I am grateful to those who gave us their time.

If my respondents are representative, thousands of Americans have reached the point where they are ready to do battle with hypocrisy. But before they can mount an effective campaign, they need a battle cry and a keen sense of who and where the enemy is. Most of all, they need a mobilizing concept, a single idea that identifies and encapsulates the many abuses. They need to understand how big faking is in America.

I.

the death of lies

ᗡ MERICA will be the first civilization to eliminate lies. Soon, in America, the lie will be superfluous, unnecessary, and will be buried.

The lie is not vanishing because it is being killed off, like some hapless species of wildlife. It is not disappearing because it was legislated out of existence, like a noxious fume, or because it has atrophied from lack of use. Clearly, lies cannot be regarded as victims of higher morality. The lie is a casualty of progress.

For the liar (who is, after all, the perpetrator of lies) the outright lie has always presented an enormous and central peril—that of being exposed, with the humiliation and even jail sentence which may follow.* So clumsy and even hazardous a weapon cried

---

* "Under normal circumstances, the liar is defeated by reality, for which there is no substitute; no matter how large the frame of falsehood that an experienced liar has to offer, it will never

out to be replaced by something that would accomplish the lie's objectives and be at the same time safe. The breakthrough has come, and as a result our society will soon be as free of lies as a diet cola is low on calories.

The new device that is making the lie obsolete can be called the Fake Factor or, for those who require still more trenchant terminology, the B.S. Factor. A factor makes or does something. Introduced into communications of any kind, this factor causes a subtle skewing of sense, a distortion of meaning, without ever becoming an actual lie. Unlike lies, which are occasional instruments used for specific purposes, the Fake Factor, to succeed, must be ubiquitous—that is, must set the standard for what is, or isn't, an acceptable level of truth. This factor, then, is responsible for a continual difference between word and reality. It has brought about the lie which is not a lie and the truth which is not the truth. Increasingly, it determines how our society talks to itself and the way it establishes meaning. Rapidly, it becomes the manner we use to project our self-image, to ourselves and others, and if it is seen as a form of counterfeiting, more and more Americans are counterfeiters.

Conventional lies wear thin sooner or later, but the Fake Factor is immensely durable, being a dense weave of logical errors and sophistries known since antiquity, combined (or recycled) into spectacular new combinations with current prejudices and inanities, defenses of failure and denials of guilt, and the modern religion of science. Besides, faking on such a scale

---

be large enough, even if he has to enlist the help of a computer, to cover the immensity of factuality."—Hannah Arendt, *New York Review*, November 18, 1971, p. 30.

is bound to cause a continual distraction of attention, which in turn protects the Fake Factor from too much scrutiny. The consequence, overall, is cant and obfuscation of such an *extent that a cerebral fog has settled upon our mental landscape, all but obliterating its real features.

Perhaps the best indication of how well fakery has succeeded is that most people seem only dimly aware, if aware at all, of how much cant their minds are compelled to absorb. Fakery, in other words, has come to seem a natural, quotidian part of experience. Indeed, that was the objective in the first place—to make the unreal appear real, the bizarre seem ordinary, the non-thing or non-person look like a thing or person, the crazy sound sane, the irregular seem regular, the distortion appear as the normal way of making a case. Because the Fake Factor is so much a part of our lives, acumen and effort are often required to detect it. Even so, the recognition can result in shock, not of the future but of the here and now.

The Fake Factor, then, has come to be an established feature of American culture, however unclear in definition our culture is, filling messageways and stores. It is brought to you in advertisements, communications, news stories. It is to be seen in the design of many products and felt in the prices of those products. It is heard on talk shows and telethons and pops up whenever a station break is announced and commercials appear instead. It resounds in the oven that plays "Tenderly" when the meat is ready, and over the Super Bowl when jet fighters swoop overhead as though the taxpayers had demanded this use of planes, pilots and fuel. It can be found in copious quantity at any stationery store—in, for instance, the daily reminders which serve as daily excuses to forget; in the ravings on license plates, like New Hampshire's LIVE FREE OR DIE; in the film ratings—"for mature audiences," meaning voyeurs; in the inflated figures for church membership; in the appliance manual's line drawing of the neat coveralled serviceman who comes when you call; in (perhaps) curiously anachronistic phrases like "Social Security" (as if security were to be found at the present rates); in sex manuals which help no one; in warranties that don't warrant; in insurance policies which insure a half of what you expected; in the folderol of the futurists; in the foofaraw of the faddists; in the barratry of book reviews; in the calumnies of columnists; in the splenetic posturings of "radicals"; in what the Pentagon Papers showed; in the prevarications of Presidential candidates and Presidents.

One way to assess the ubiquity and impact of the Fake Factor is to ask what happens in its absence—for without a generous application of fakery, TV ratings can fall, grants may not come through, exams may be flunked, candidates may lose, income-tax returns may be penalized. Skill at faking will not automatically guarantee success, but it will take one—even one deficient in other talents—a long way toward the pinnacle.

The cumulative fakery which adds up to something big in our cultural context has not gone unnoticed. Let us quote from merely a few of the social commentators who have remarked on the phenomenon. Murray Kempton: "People confront a world now where all the information they get seems to be misinformation." Richard Goodwin: "the limitless fog of deception and illusion which has numbed the citizen." Cleanth

Brooks: "Ours is a time when cant is spoken and heard everywhere." M. C. Goodall: "We live in a carefully hedged system of small lies and fake images." Hannah Arendt: "I feel like we're living in a fairy tale. The country has fallen under a spell and nothing seems to work anymore." Still, fakery is employed more than ever.

The Fake Factor is usually expressed in words, and vocabulary for this reason is a major ingredient. Dr. Johnson observed that when grammarians discuss the problems of the world they reduce them to problems of grammar. Notwithstanding, the language is revealing about the workings of the Fake Factor, one effect being what it does *to* words. Words by the thousands have been affected and even undone; at times it seems that the whole vocabulary is unraveling like a loosely knit sweater. The language flies apart. Speech has always been a way for the individual to adjust to his environment and restore his own equilibrium, but because of widespread fakery disequilibrium is constant.

Let us begin with a few examples which may at first seem petty and superfluous. Bear in mind, though, that language is the key to thought. I have a gadget—a real gadget—with three speed settings: FAST, INFINITE SPEED, and SLO. Forget about the missing w and concentrate a moment on INFINITE SPEED. It isn't enough that this pathetic piece of equipment is claimed to have a part which moves as fast as or faster than light. INFINITE SPEED must also be tucked between FAST and SLO: "infinite" as a word has been *destroyed* in this context. "Contemporary News on American Contemporary Radio." News that is not contemporary would be "history." "Free gifts." What is a gift if it isn't free? "New improved." How can something new be improved? A whole class of usage resembles these examples.

It will be objected (wrongly) that such word-boning (A) springs from ignorance, (B) develops out of a commercial matrix where it can always be expected, and (C) doesn't matter in the first place. Objection (A) assumes an ignorance so profound that no one remembers gifts are free or the meaning of "infinite"; it fails to account for the considerable cleverness displayed by the new vocabulary. Objection (B) is easily disposed of by the prevalence of reverse English where commercial considerations are minor or nonexistent. "Project Apollo"—aimed for the moon but named for the sun. "Re-entry"—but how can a space capsule re-enter that which it has left but not yet entered? Does "stationary learning stand" improve on "desk"? Can a "Peace Fighter" be a military aircraft? Does "idle" describe the unemployed? "Operation Phoenix" —the bird Phoenix was reborn peacefully out of its own ashes; "Operation Phoenix" burned huts in Vietnam and accounted for the slaughter of countless civilians.

As for Objection (C), that sleight-of-mouth doesn't matter: it does. The verbal concoctions dripping from our lips can easily lead to illusion and error, and result in the inflamed rhetoric and unceasing cant of our day. Words are means of *doing* things, and chaos in language brings chaos in deed. A good (and by no means irrelevant) parallel to what has been happening to language can be found in industrial design. A detailed book on the subject cites dozens of examples of overwrought, overelaborated designs which inundate the marketplace.* The same trend is to be observed in language: toward ever-greater use of euphemism, hyperbole, and very often the completely meaningless. The waste characteristic of modern design is also found in the uses of language—the same slicked-up *kitsch* performs for both. And the end toward which both the language and design seem to proceed is the same: a sterile, compartmentalized, standardized, technological environment, choking in fluff.

"The confusion of tongues can have practical consequences. . . . If you debauch a language you run a grave risk of debauching the minds of those who use it," remarks Cleanth Brooks.† One of the main results of continual fakery is confusion—confusion about objectives, means, ends, and meanings. Nor does this confusion seem coincidental. It might be compared to a protective screen behind which Americans can hide their fears, their failures, their true preoccupations, the obsolescence of some of their polar ideas, the selfishness of interest groups, the shortcomings of their society. The language seems to speak of false bravado, of spurious technological romanticism and a deification of science, of a superiority complex, of an increasingly regimented form of life, and, most loudly of all, of self-delusion. To fake, then, in language and logic, is a way of appearing to make contradictions square, or of burying them altogether in the haze of splintered intellect.

Let us take an example from business. As a red-

---

* Victor Papanek, *Design for the Real World, Human Ecology and Social Change,* with an introduction by R. Buckminster Fuller, New York: Pantheon Books, 1971.
† "Telling It Like It Is in the Tower of Babble," *The Sewanee Review,* Winter, 1971, pp. 136–38.

blooded American businessman, you might say (in fact, you *do* say) that the American business system is historically unique. But you also claim that free enterprise is natural to human beings. Logically, it is impossible to have it both ways. Either free enterprise as practiced here is unique, in which case it can hardly be called natural, or it is natural, in which case it is not unique. Rather than facing up to the contradiction, the temptation is to summon what the sociologist C. Wright Mills called sponge words—such as "freedom"—which soak up the inconsistency.

> Freedom of action is our way of life. Our progress has been founded on individual initiative, ingenuity and freedom of action. A free competitive economy is based on individual ambition which is the most universal, reliable and powerful of human motives.*

The effect of this statement is to make the American business environment (free enterprise) seem rational, necessary, and beneficent. The contradiction has been, if not resolved, then pushed out of sight through the use of both "individual" and "universal." But observe that no lie has been uttered—merely obfuscation. Now take a statement from the National Association of Broadcasters which, no doubt, had the frequent attacks on the quality of television in mind.

> Television is seen and heard in every type of American home. These homes include children and adults of all ages, embrace all races and all varieties of religious faith, and reach those of every educational background. It is the responsibility of

---

* National Association of Manufacturers, Manual of Official Policy Positions, January 1, 1967, p. 82.

television to bear constantly in mind that the audience is primarily a home audience, and conse-
quently that television's relationship to the viewers
is that between guest and host.

The revenues from advertising support the free,
competitive American system of telecasting, and
make available to the eyes and ears of the
American people the finest programs of information, education, culture and entertainment . . .
the broadcaster . . . is obliged to bring his posi-
tive responsibility for excellence and good taste in
programming to bear.

Television and all who participate in it are
jointly accountable to the American public for
respect for the special needs of children, for community responsibility, for the advancement of the
program materials chosen, for decency and decorum
in production, and for property in advertising. This
responsibility cannot be discharged by any given
group of programs but can be discharged only
through the highest standards of respect for the
American home, applied to every moment of every
program presented by television.*

The unwillingness to come to grips with the problem
of TV quality is positively awesome. Fakery has been
used successfully to skirt the issue through language
as slippery as cornstarch, without the resort to outright
lies. But just to prove that faking is not the province of
trade associations alone, let us note an entirely different use of it.

Consider the notion, frequently expressed by New
York City politicians, that New York's drug addicts steal
between two and five billion dollars' worth of property
a year to "sustain their habit." It is simply never asked
—because only the impact of the statement is thought

---

* Code, dated August, 1968.

to matter—whether such a frightening claim is *true*. Accuracy is the enemy of the Fake Factor. The enormous spread between two and five billion is a clear indication that something is wrong with the statistics. And a clearheaded analysis shows that even the two-billion figure is hugely inflated, perhaps by a factor of ten.* Admittedly, there can exist honest disagreements on matters of fact (and also straightforward opinions which turn out to be wrong). Just the same, the eagerness to admit something into evidence before its validity is properly established is another characteristic of faking it.

Invariably, of course, the Fake Factor is used for effect, and it helps account for the thinness of the contemporary political language. Consider the following:

> We stand at a crossroad in our history. We shall reaffirm our destiny for greatness or we shall choose instead to withdraw into ourselves. A nation needs many qualities but it needs faith and confidence above all. Skeptics do not build societies. The idealists are the builders . . . every man achieves his own greatness by reaching out beyond himself. And so it is with nations.
>
> —RICHARD NIXON

Little or nothing in this utterance can be backed up by evidence or logic of any kind. Did God give sanction to the "destiny for greatness"? What is "greatness"? The "choice" does not pose mutually exclusive alternatives and is thus a choice in rhetoric only. That "skeptics do not build societies" is, to say the least, uncertain of proof. The identification of the actions of men and na-

---

* Max Singer, "The Vitality of Mythical Numbers," *The Public Interest,* Spring, 1971, pp. 3–9.

tions is both a rhetorical trick and a logical fallacy—the identification of a whole with its parts.

The temptation (and there is always the temptation) will be to dismiss the various deficiencies and inconsistencies in such utterances as being necessary (for what is never explained) and somehow normal, as though what is said and what is done need bear no very close relation ("Watch what we do, not what we say"). But on closer look, the failures of the rhetoric relate closely to failures in the design and logic of policy. The greater the logical lapses in a social policy, the more the rhetoric must be stretched to cover them. In the spring of 1972 the President defended the blockade (though it wasn't called that) and air war against North Vietnam by saying that the issue was "the position of the United States as the strongest nation in the world." At the same time, the United States was withdrawing troops from the South. As *Time* pointed out, "By all logic, if so much is at stake in Vietnam, his disengagement could be considered grossly negligent. [Nixon] ought to be pouring U.S. troops into the conflict, rather than pulling them out of it."

The difficulty here seems to have been that the President confronted two conflicting imperatives—one being the political necessity of continuing the withdrawal and the second that (rightly or wrongly) he did not want to lose the war. The contradictions in the policy led immediately to the contradictions and overstatements of the rhetoric; in just this way, faking springs out of the larger contradictions and distortions in American life. The greater the role of fakery, the greater the problems beneath.

It would be wrong, then, to put the blame for the Fake Factor on political parties, occupational groups, or specific individuals. If President Nixon deployed it, he was only doing what Presidents Johnson and Kennedy had done before him. Nor are the usual scapegoats entirely responsible—advertising, public relations, image-makers, sales people, market research, TV, the bureaucracy, the military-industrial complex. To fake it appears to be a product of American culture itself. *All* of us feel, whether we admit it or not, that hypocrisy is necessary for survival—social and personal.

One more proof of how vital we consider the Big Fake is the price we are willing to pay for it. Faking more or less dictates that suspicion will rule, for who can be certain, in a world of half-truths, just what is real? It demands mediocrity because it diminishes intelligence. It leads to waste: material waste (in tangible social products) and people-waste, the waste of time and the loss of being. To tell lies, at least, a knowledge of truth is required, and as lying atrophies so does the sense of truth. Truth and lies become indistinguishable.

This polemic is not a brief for "truth." As H. L. Mencken churlishly but sensibly said, "The man who boasts that he habitually tells the truth is simply a man with no respect for it. It is not a thing to be thrown around loosely, like small change; it is something to be cherished and hoarded and disbursed only when absolutely necessary." But it is a brief for a harder look at reality and ourselves, which means a choice:

Either we continue to resort to fakery, wallowing around in half-truths and mindless nonsense, ignoring the issue of hypocrisy, bolstering our economy with the waste that the Fake Factor feeds on, permitting our international standing to decline further, and eventually reducing ourselves to mental vegetables in suburban gardens,

Or we develop into a race of satirists and diamond-hard skeptics (as should be our inheritance), asking sharp questions about not only what we say but also what we do and who we are. If it turns out that we are a nation of cheats and crooks, barbarians in business suits, let us at least face the reality. Clearly—whatever else is true of us—Americans are a people deeply deeply mired in their own rhetoric. To get on solid ground will mean to carry on a nonviolent struggle against deception wherever it appears, in institutions and in people. Even more than clean streets, we need clear heads.

II.

new directions in cant

To FACILITATE examination of the Fake Factor, we may break it down into styles or "systems" of thought and language.* Instead of merely crying "fraud" and switching channels, it is better to know the components of the Fake Factor—especially as it will be found on the other channels, too.

The categories presented here are descriptive and arbitrary; others could have been chosen. You might do better inventing ones of your own, and you will be tempted. Mine have to do partly with style, partly with language, and partly with content. They are in alphabetical order, and a limited time with them will give you, perhaps, an insight into faking as it lurks behind the headlines, pamphlets, claims, political speeches, or

---

* And also to save "bullshit" from premature exhaustion. Those who overuse it know that something is wrong but can't define what it is—hence, "Booolllsheeet!" at every turn.

as it lies deep in our practices and mentality. I have tried to make the categories, as the logicians say, "discrete," but overlap is unavoidable. Life is not a matter of neat distinctions.

Some of the systems are intended as more serious in implication than others. Not everybody expresses all of them, but enough partake in enough of them to count. Assemble them in any combination or permutation and you have the essential elements of the Fake Factor.

Americant

Patriotism is no vice. Star-spangled Americant is:

> Ours is the most advanced, most productive, richest, and most powerful society that humanity has seen since the dawn of history. What were the key elements in the formula we have followed which allowed us—in the brief span of two centuries—to raise up on this continent a Nation which is a model for the world and a credit to mankind?
>
> It was freedom—freedom to work and to worship—to learn—to choose—to fashion the best life attainable with individual initiative, imagination and courage.
>
> It was an unfettered, free enterprise economic system that delivered to each man and woman the rewards they earned.
>
> —SENATOR JAMES O. EASTLAND

Users of such Americant deserve to be hung by their rhetoric. Consider the habit of talking about the country as though it were in its brawny adolescence. No other democracy has existed so long. The very people who rave about America as though it were an infant in swaddling clothes are also the ones who invoke the longevity of our institutions to prove our superiority.

Another habit is to make Americant serve as umbrella for things that deserve to stand separately.

It is no historical accident that Democracy, the United States of America and Capitalism were all born in the latter half of the eighteenth century. The hour for them had struck. Together they developed and today, welded into the great entity of Democratic American Capitalism, they dominate the world. Still so welded they should mold the future.*

Remember the American Century, Pax Americana, and such?

American claims to superiority involve a logical dilemma—to prove your superiority you have to define your terms and make sure they are universal; anything less is to leave yourself open to charges of thickheadedness, boasting, being a bully, covering up a national inferiority complex, etc.—but we have been so heavily indoctrinated with Americant that we can't quite scuttle it for a more modest self-appraisal. One tenet of the American faith clearly remains unshaken: what the Irish scholar Conor Cruise O'Brien calls "Americanocentrism," the belief that the world not only loves America but thinks about it every moment. Why, there is rumored to be a man in Tasmania who has not thought about America since 1934!

The red-white-and-blue picture show is fine to watch —"The decor for this Flag Day wedding ceremony [of Defense Secretary Melvin Laird's daughter] was red, white and blue. Red and white roses cover[ed] the altar of the big red-brick church. . . . The bride's attendants completed the color scheme with navy-colored gowns. . . . [Others] wore colonial picture hats, navy silk

---

* Ernest L. Klein, *How to Stay Rich*. New York: Farrar, Straus, 1960, p. 189. Quoted in Francis X. Sutton, Seymour E. Harris, Carl Keysen, James Tobin, *The American Business Creed*. New York: Schocken Books (paper), 1962, p. 37.

organza gowns and carried red and white roses"—but there is often something aggressive about Americant too, as though Americans were still fighting the British. In any case, the Marines still use Americant to stir up the farm boys.

THE RIFLEMAN'S CREED

This is my rifle. There are many like it, but this one is mine.

My rifle is my best friend. It is my life. I must master it as I master my life.

My rifle, without me, is useless. Without my rifle I am useless. I must fire my rifle true. I must shoot straighter than my enemy who is trying to kill me. I will . . .

My rifle is human, even as I, because it is my life. Thus, I will learn it as a brother. . . . We will become part of each other.

We will . . .

Before God I swear this creed. My rifle and myself are the defenders of my country. We are the masters of our enemy. We are the saviors of my life.

So be it, until victory is America's and there is no enemy, but Peace!

—UNITED STATES MARINE CORPS MANUAL

Is Peace the enemy?

Amerikant

The kurious habit of spelling Amerika with a "k"—as in Ku Klux Klan—is kharakteristik of Amerikant. This is meant to be a kolossal insult. The trouble is that those who affekt to spell Amerika with a "k" engage in reasoning fully as cirkular as that of the patriots who oppose them. Whereas, to the latter, America is great, therefore Americans are great, therefore America is great, etc., for the Amerikant buff the traffik moves in the opposite direktion. Either way, the trip goes nowhere. The fallacy lies in thinking that what is true of a part is true of the whole.

Amerikant leads easily to blaming America (or the "American system") for everything wrong in the world. Every petty tyrant, every reaction, every war is the fault of America (or the CIA). This exaggerated notion of American influence over the world is quite as Americanocentric as that of those who believe in our "total global responsibility," as a high-ranking State Department official once put it. Nor do the champions of Amerikant give credit to the democratic luxuries we do have.

> The state forbids any person to use democratic freedoms to the detriment of the interests of the state and of the people.
> —NORTH VIETNAMESE CONSTITUTION OF 1960

A simple answer to Amerikant and Americant is to return to the older, less evocative, more accurate term for America, the United States. "United States" is harder to say and will therefore be used less frequently than "America," which would be a blessing. And you can't spell "United States" with a "k." (See also Undistributed Outlook.)

Anarchlings

Anarchlings are not quite so bold as anarchists. A real anarchist rebels against any and all kinds of authority and/or he believes in a system that has never been tested: self-government without established political institutions. The anarchling, or little anarchist, is merely in flight from mass society and all its works.

One kind of anarchling is to be found sipping carrot juice at a health bar during his lunch hour, with a copy of *The Last Whole Earth Catalog* under his arm. He might earn $30,000 a year and have his children in private schools, but he dreams of making his own goat cheese by candlelight. The Crunchy Granola, whole-grain bread, unrefined honey, unsulfured fruit, super-fresh eggs, cold-pressed oils, natural ice cream, organic vegetables, and various macrobiotic delicacies he picks up at a Natural Food Shoppe (yes, "Shoppe"—I swear it) are his way of casting a vote against mass production.*

---

* "If the government has not actively 'gone after' the health-food industry, it is only because proof of fraud is difficult and costly to come by, and in any case, these foods are not in any way harmful. But the official attitude is nowhere more apparent than in an FDA fact sheet issued to help consumers evaluate health-food claims. It suggests the incredible test

You don't have to defend the present practices of food production to see that "natural" rests on an erroneous concept. To put "natural" in opposition to "man-made" implies that "man-made" is not "natural." But this is to put an additive into "natural," since whatever is *is* "natural" (except to those who have larded the word with their own values and concepts). For the anarchlings, the enemy of the "natural" is the machine.

The hatred of machines can be called neo-Ludditism. The Luddites were a group of early-nineteenth-century British workmen who reacted to the introduction of machines by attempting to destroy them. Today's Luddites have not reached the point of attacking computers with crowbars, but they place great faith in the idea of doing it yourself, without machinery if possible and even when faintly impossible.

Anarchlings speak anarchese:

> this book is for people who would rather chop wood than work behind a desk so they can pay P.G.&E. [Pacific Gas and Electric Company]. it has no chapters; it just grew as I learned; you may find the index your only guide to this unmapped land. however, if you have a feeling for the flow of things, you will discover a path: from traveling the wilds to the first fence, simple housing, furnishing houses, crafts, agriculture, food preparation, medicine—not unlike the development of our ancient ancestors. when we depend less on industrially produced consumer goods, we can live in quiet places. our bodies become vigorous; we dis-

question 'Does the promoter belittle normal foods? This is the first sign of nutritional quackery.' . . ." As the writer asks, are TV dinners "normal"? "A Skeptic's Guide to Health Food Stores," Mimi Sheraton, *New York,* May 8, 1972, p. 48.

> cover the serenity of living with the rhythms of
> the earth. we cease oppressing one another.*

Before they abide on the earth, rural anarchlings would do well to live awhile in a library. It is a simple-minded and boring notion that living in tune with the "rhythms of the earth" brings vigor and health and ends oppression. The most cursory reading of human history says the opposite. But the standards of the rural anarchling are not based on history; he measures worth almost entirely by degree of deviation from standard culture. For him, things are good in themselves when they are *harder* and *take longer*.

I happen to detest rural life, but I can see how some might enjoy it. The pastoral vision of the anarchlings, though, contains the seeds of a primitive philosophy or even a religion. Its articles of faith are that time is endless (which helps account perhaps for the bovine expressions of rural anarchlings), that machines are barely necessary, and that the battle over scarcity has been won. When the rural anarchlings gather in their serious-minded "communes," they discover the terrible truth. Without machinery and a profitable activity, they cannot be economically self-sufficient. So they take their homemade jams and cracked corn and move to the cities.

The urban anarchling is in somewhat worse shape than his country cousin, and can sometimes be found reduced to a completely dependent position—begging. (He may not think begging is dependency, but it is.) Banded with his fellows in crowded pads, he will tell you that life is cool. Consider, however, the terror that

---

* alicia bay laurel, *living on the earth*. new york: vintage books, random house, 1971 (unpaginated, of course).

lurks behind the "most needed" telephone listings in an underground newspaper:

> ACLU, Air Pollution Control Center, County Hospital, Draft Counseling, Fire Department, Legal Aid, Mental Health Clinic, Council for a New Politics, Outside-In Clinic, Planned Parenthood, Poison Center, Rumor Control Center, Suicide Prevention, VD Clinic, Water Pollution Authority, Tear Gas and Mace Distribution.

Sooner or later, the urban anarchling is forced to find work—usually, and oddly, in the retail business—and from then on it's *The Last Whole Earth Catalog* and the health-food bar.

Many otherwise thoughtful people believe that our society slouches toward the day when two hundred million Americans will anarchically depart from the productive apparatus, rousing themselves from pot-induced torpor only long enough to eat and fornicate. But a massive withdrawal from industrial life could result in strangulation of the cities and starvation of their people. If necessary, millions of potheads in hard hats will be driven to work with whips. (There will always be plenty of people who will gladly wield the whips.)

Anything Authorities

The thirst for answers in a difficult world has brought the rise of Anything (or Everything) Authorities. The Anything Authority is one whose credentials in one field are taken as valid for others—sometimes many others. Examples are Dr. George Wald, the biologist; Dr. Benjamin Spock, the pediatrician; Jane Fonda, the actress —all of whom are Anything Authorities on war, peace, and politics—and Dr. Linus Pauling, who said of President Nixon, "For fifteen years I have studied insanity. I saw the eyes on television, and there is madness, paranoia." (Dr. Pauling has worked on the molecular basis of mental disease, including schizophrenia, but that's a far cry from diagnostics based on a picture on a screen.)

The trouble with an Anything Authority is not that he takes a position or works for a cause but that he seldom seems to apply the same standards of research and documentation to the field in which he is not expert as he would to his own. (Since many Anything Authorities are scientists, the ineluctable suspicion must be that scientists do not regard the field of international relations, say, as anything worthy of special knowledge.) The opinions of Dr. Pauling, twice winner of the Nobel Prize, once for Chemistry and once for Peace, must always be respected, and yet it is difficult to imagine Pauling discussing the double helix in quite the glib manner he used for his discovery of Nixon's paranoia.* In his own discipline the authority must qualify and prove. Such requirements vanish when the topic is anything.

Psychiatrists are a special breed of Anything Authorities because their field is anything (or almost) in the first place. Psychiatrists have been handed the license to give the news media instant diagnoses of people they have never met, much less analyzed. ("Manson embodies the demonic characteristics which are in all of us but seldom come out," a psychiatrist told the press. When was your demon last heard from?)

When an Anything Authority becomes successful, he joins the Permanent Rotating Panel Show and appears on television programs, which pay him. Besides fame as an Anything Authority, there are two criteria for membership on the PRPS. One is that the audience reacts—whether with cheers or boos doesn't matter—and the other is that the Anything Authority must *never* be stuck for an answer. Glibness helps, and so does the fact that many emcees do not know the hard questions to ask.

Anything Authorities are in great demand—quoted in print, called upon to write book reviews, invited to join boards of directors to add panache, given sizable per diems as consultants, and used for all manner of fund drives. Anything Authorities exist because there is still hope that somebody still knows something outside narrow fields of specialization—despite abundant evidence to the contrary.

---

* Dr. Pauling is, however, a serious student of peace and has fought hard for reductions in nuclear weapons and against the Vietnam war.

Apocalese

> Between the close of the eleventh century and the
> first half of the sixteenth it repeatedly happened in
> Europe that the desire of the poor to improve the
> material conditions of their lives became transfused
> with phantasies of a new Paradise on earth, a world
> purged of suffering and sin, a Kingdom of Saints.
> —NORMAN COHN, *In Pursuit of the Millennium**

In a country so prideful of its pragmatism, many are
believers in the apocalypse. The future, to the apocalyptic, is revealed. The end of the earth is upon us unless
drastic action is taken *at once*. Like the medieval
Manichee, the American apocalyptic preaches a simple
dualism and explains the miseries of the world.

One feature of Apocalese is an almost total despair
because the millennium has not already arrived. ("The
world is absolutely out of control now, and it is not
going to be saved by reason or unreason."—Robert
Lowell) Another is the notion of the perpetual crisis
against which the brave man pits himself, to serve humanity and, importantly, to prove his heroism. Note that
the author of the next quotation is Father Daniel Ber-
rigan, S.J., who went to prison for burning draft cards.

---

* New York: Harper Torchbooks, 1961, p. xiii.

> Drama is the purifying clash of spiritual forces; a struggle which is intensely personal but which still implies immediate and explosive social consequences. In tragic drama, the defeat of the hero is the prelude to his victory, and heroism is an achievement won from the deepest reaches of suffering. At the outcome of the tragedy, man stands renewed in his being, in acceptance of his identity as son and brother. The hero has won a definition that is both genetic and final. Man's victory over egoism and the forces of evil restores him to the original form willed by God—a form postulated by man's deeper instincts, deformed by sin, and finally restored in Christ. But his new identity also makes him a man of the future, *a sign of the last day.**

Both these attitudes combine with a third, the attempt to publicize the cause. Minority positions, such as the apocalyptics usually occupy, cannot get sufficient support merely by promising God's blessing. They must also assert that failure to achieve mass conversion will result in the fire next time. Anything short of a final solution (one way or the other) is ignored by the apocalyptics, because it doesn't satisfy personal urges and/or because not enough people will listen—or so it is believed.

The apocalyptic argument has become a constant in political thought. Only the nature of the imminent apocalypse changes. Either there is total nuclear disarmament or the world will be destroyed, argued the peace movement a decade ago. Today it is tin cans, smog, the population explosion, resources.

> The principal defect of the industrial way of life with its ethos of expansion is that it is not sustain-

---

* *They Call Us Dead Men: Reflections on Life and Conscience.* New York: Macmillan, 1966, p. 25. (Italics added.)

able. Its termination within the lifetime of someone
born today is inevitable—unless it continues to be
sustained for a while longer by an entrenched minority at the cost of imposing great suffering on the
rest of mankind.

—*The Ecologist* (Great Britain)

Or, in the American version:

There may be no realistic hope of the present
underdeveloped countries reaching the standard of
living demonstrated by the present industrialized
nations. . . . Noting the destruction that has already occurred on land, in the air, and especially in
the oceans, capability appears not to exist for handling such a rise in standard of living. In fact, the
present disparity between the developed and underdeveloped nations may be equalized as much by a
decline in the developed countries as by an im-
provement in the underdeveloped countries.

A society with a high level of industrialization
may be nonsustainable. It may be self-extinguish-
ing if it exhausts the natural resources on which it
depends. Or, if unending substitution for declining
natural resources were possible, a new international strife over pollution and environmental
rights might pull the average world-wide standard
of living back to the level of a century ago.*

Frequently, the apocalyptic argument can be distinguished by its naïveté, revealed by its dogmatic acceptance of speculations as fact in its rush to judgment, and by its quest for high drama. Issues like
nuclear arms and the "environment" are real enough;
the question is whether the apocalyptic attitude helps.
Perhaps the apocalyptics are reacting to a narrow, self-

---

* Jay W. Forrester, *World Dynamics*. Cambridge, Mass.:
Wright-Allen Press, 1971, p. 12.

serving pragmatism which put the world in its present situation. But the apocalyptic is a pessimist about the ability of men to change their lot.

Big-Timing

From childhood, Americans are taught to admire big-ness for itself.

> THE WORLD'S BIGGEST SCULPTURES
> *The Mount Rushmore National Memorial*
> *South Dakota*
> These presidential heads in stone
> Are quite the largest ever known;
> The giant noses, mouths and eyes
> Are 8o times their natural sizes,
> If you like heads, you'll get your quota
> Way out there in South Dakota.
> —*the pop-up biggest book*

The bigness binge continues throughout life, always on the assumption that quantity proves quality: the length of a book (regardless of how much it has to say), the square footage of a building (even if it's half unoccupied), the record-breaking budget (no matter how much waste is involved), the amount of a prize (ignoring the odds of winning it), the rate of acquisition (so profits are falling), the size of a sex organ (never mind if it's hot or cold), the extent of an empire (without questioning what purpose it serves). It follows that smallness is bad (except when larger things have been miniaturized successfully, like a mechanical component). One Congressman complained bitterly over a Federal arts grant for a poem on the ground that it was too tiny: one word.*

Big-Timing is at bottom inflationary. As such, it leads straight to a Big-Time Style—poised, affluent, achieving, multinational, confident, aggressive, growth-oriented, and "thinking big." The sort of word the Big-Timers admire is "power." Big-Timing put a capital "P" on President—always lower-case before. That was because the President of America had power; it was constantly reiterated that he was "the most powerful man in the world."

A typical Big-Timer is McGeorge Bundy, President of the Ford Foundation. A photograph shows him at work, feet up, casual, fingers tapping the desk top as he talks. Bundy is impatient—his "steel-trap" mind can absorb, collate, and evaluate information faster than the speaker can spit it out. Three TV sets in his office enable him to catch three television programs simultaneously and not miss a word even as he pours water from the water cooler and coffee from a coffeepot. From his swivel chair, arched like a catapult, Bundy is ready to spring to battle. He is "actively promoting social change," says the caption. Perhaps he was misguided in urging the bombing of North Vietnam, but no one suggested that he might take a few months to "rethink."†

---

* The poem was by Aram Saroyan; the word, a neologism, was "lighght." The Congressman was Representative Scherle of Iowa.

† "It is the great merit of the proposed scheme [a policy of "sustained reprisal" against North Vietnam] that to stop it the Communists would have to stop enough of their activity in the South to permit the probable success of a determined pacification effort," Bundy wrote in 1965. (*The Pentagon Papers* as published by *The New York Times*. New York: Bantam Books, 1971,

Big-Timing has a Larger-than-Life quality: Larger-than-Life people, power, country, visions, dreams. . . . Fort Knox; airborne round-the-clock command-and-control systems; an entire air base inside a mountain. Astrodomes, big-time money, conglomerates, big planes —nothing's too great for the boys, who after all were taught that self-esteem depends on size.

---

p. 389.) Wrote Townsend Hoopes, "Bundy was a brilliant and self-assured pragmatist of the highest ability. . . . In a fundamental sense he was a process man who, aware of the unforeseeable ways in which events not yet born will impinge upon and alter preselected courses of action, believes that what is important is to get started in the right direction and play it by ear." (*The Limits of Intervention.* New York: David McKay Co., 1969, pp. 19–20.)

Candor Con

These days, almost everybody is pledged to divulge the truth and nothing but the truth, while finding his opponents less than completely open. Product advertisements and Presidential candidates both insist their labels are accurate while those of the others are not. "Truth is a habit of integrity, not a strategy of politics," said Senator George McGovern. President Nixon pledged his first administration to "complete candor."

Repeated use of the Candor Con reveals a deeply cynical view about the judgment of others. You know perfectly well that complete candor is generally undesirable and/or impossible, yet you want others to think that you are completely candid. It follows that the more you pitch for total truth the more you deserve to be distrusted, whether you are a preacher, a business leader, or the President.

Revealing an infantile streak in our culture, many quest for total truth and actually believe they are getting it because somebody claims to be handing it out. A fear of artifice and a distrust of disingenuousness spring from a simple-minded supposition that an artful approach to reality (even one that avoids fakery) is somehow wrong. The results may be heavy-handedness and naiveté, leading to premature and massive loss of

confidence on the part of those who eventually feel
they have been victimized. Complete openness is a
dream, but the hunger for total truth persists, and anyone who wants to deal with the American public must
come to grips with it, be he the basest of fakers.

Cheaters

Leafing through Rod Laver's *Education of a Tennis Player*, I ran across the following:

> I was stunned myself when Dave Anderson of *The New York Times* tape-measured me one afternoon in 1968 and reported that my left forearm is twelve inches around—as big as Rocky Marciano's was. And my left wrist is seven inches around. Floyd Patterson, another heavyweight champion, had a six-inch wrist.

I was busy wondering how Laver's arm could have been measured *except* with a tape, and whether the results would have been different in the morning from what they were in the afternoon, when, one evening, I got my own tape measure off the shelf and wrapped it around my seemingly normal wrist and forearm. The measurements were about the same.

Cheaters refers to a wide world of petty deceptions resting on ruses. It isn't admitted when in lotteries the winning numbers are picked in advance, so that, if nobody claims a prize, it simply isn't given. (In some lotteries only ten per cent of the prizes are awarded.) "Fourth printing sold out!" How large were the first three? "No. 1 Best Seller," but the real best sellers

(Bibles, cookbooks, *The Prophet*, etc.) often don't make the charts at all. Dinty Moore—"NFL Official Training Table Stew"—doesn't say whether it paid (much less how much) for the franchise.

Cheaters of an obvious kind are TV commercials: paste "ice cream," drinks iced by plastic cubes, "coffee" and "tea" made of colored water, steam produced by air brush, drinks that fizz because a tablet has been dropped into them, fake fruit and flowers, surfaces that look polished thanks to graphite, foods cooked before they are placed in the appliances . . . well, you can't expect them to use real ice cubes because they melt under the lights. Still, only a small step is needed to get from the ice cube to the soup thickened with marbles or the portable TV set the skinny model can pick up with a finger because it has no insides. From there, it's another little jump to the claim of the TV industry that the commercials are no louder than the programs (as if nobody had ears), and so on and so on—to the B.S. spectaculars of modern life.*

What does it matter if Carter Burden, during his successful campaign for the New York City Council, sent out a letter to Democrats saying he was a former legislative aide to Senator Robert F. Kennedy and another to Republicans calling himself a former legislative aide to an unnamed U.S. Senator? Samuel Johnson, pondering a similarly negligible slip by an English poet (Congreve) about where he was born, puzzled

---

* E. William Henry, former Chairman of the Federal Communications Commission, tells this story: "We members of the FCC were given a demonstration by the TV industry to prove that the volume of the commercials was not and could not be louder than the regular programs. On the way out I asked a technician seated at a large console how he would make the commercials louder if he wanted to. 'Why,' said the technician, 'I turn this knob.'"

over why it made any difference. There were, Johnson decided, "falsehoods of convenience and vanity, falsehoods from which no evil immediately ensues *except the general degradation of human testimony. . . .*"

Complex Complex

If you have a Complex Complex, you have a compulsion to make things more complicated than they need to be, or to find a complex solution for what may be a simple problem.

The Complex Complex is revealed in an infatuation with technology, a perfectionistic urge to be able to deal with all contingencies, a desire to display knowledge, a hatred of simplicity, etc. Those with a good case of the Complex Complex are usually willing to spend money—someone else's. The result is more of everything, from missiles to chrome, from fancy designs to higher prices. Why settle for less when you can get more? is the general idea.

The Complex Complex can be used as a rhetorical device. The theory is: eschew simple answers in favor of complicated ones to muddy the issue (which is not the same as loading an argument with many points— see Many Points). Casper W. Weinberger, when on the Nixon White House staff, demonstrated the technique. About consumerism he said, ". . . a lot of people are trying to utilize consumerism to secure a more drastic result, the acceptance of the idea that our capitalist system just won't work and never will work." By giving consumerism (better goods at lower prices) more complex objectives than it sought or wanted, Weinberger made it sound subversive.

People with a Complex Complex are often at home in the law. Lawyers write laws which are resolutely complex. One reason the laws are complex is to make them impossible to read—hence, the need for lawyers.

> When litter is in the immediate vicinity of an individual and that individual has other property in his immediate possession which is of the same brand name, such person or persons shall be presumed to have caused the litter to be abandoned in the immediate vicinity. (Proposed Riverhead, Long Island, town law)

The Complex Complex figures in insurance policies, guarantees, warranties, medical-care plans, etc., making it harder to collect. In corporate reports, complicated wording, fine print, and footnotes are hardly learning aids to what is going on. ("The smaller the footnotes, the closer the approaching financial problems," warns Lewis Gilbert, a crusader for corporate honesty.) The Complex Complex is entrenched at the Department of Defense and in its weapons systems. Unfortunately, the Russians have a Complex Complex too. (See also Hyperrationality.)

Copy Cant

Few people will take a flier on a prototype when it's new and untested, but when a prototype succeeds everybody wants to copy it. What wasn't a cliché to start with rapidly becomes one, and then even clichés are copied.

Copy Cant is familiar in advertising (no wonder copywriters are called *copy* writers), but it is more prevalent than is generally realized in fields that take pride in their intellectuality. Consider the title chains of books. Betty Friedan's *The Feminine Mystique* had such a tiny print order and low visibility that *The New York Times Book Review* did not review it. (True, a newspaper strike was in progress, but the *Times* caught up with other books.) "Mystique" became popular and soon mothered a dozen books with "mystique" in their titles: *Jewish, Southern, Masculine*, etc. David Riesman's *The Lonely Crowd* (also neglected by the *Times*), brought out the "crowd" books. Richard Rovere's *The American Establishment* established "establishment" in titles, just as Charles Schultz's *Happiness Is a Warm Puppy* sired a litter of "happiness is" titles.

Copy Cant applies to style and content, too, as in fashions and movies. Such is the lack of originality

in many mod films that it is sometimes hard to remember which one you are seeing. Nor is education
immune from Copy Cant, as when Cooper Union offers
courses like "Up from the Ghetto," "The Quest for
Relevance," "The Paradox of Communication." Listen
to "New Detroit" with its "problem of communication":
"Communication between black and white. Communication between the powerful and the alienated." Will
communication with the powerful get you a Cadillac?
Even a Ford? Words and concepts like "communication," "alienation," "relevance," "ghetto," "involvement"
may have had authority to start with but by the time
they've been worked to death they're no guide to anything except yawning and staying home. (See Fadthink and Image Words.)

Counterculturism

A counterculture is not, as innocents might suppose, the culture of sandwich shops, but the culture of opposition to American culture. The Counterculturists tend to beg the question whether there *is* an American culture which you can be counter to.

One of the most notable features of our culture is the high degree of uncertainty about what it is and isn't (as reflected, for instance, in the sharply differing accounts of the culture). Again and again, the culture tries to reassure itself that it *is* a culture. One of the best ways is to find a culture that is in opposition to *the* culture, which helps establish the existence of *the* culture. Therefore, American culture not only welcomes the counterculture but even tries to take credit for it. (". . . this new cultural phase has evolved naturally—and to some extent even intentionally—out of the preceding phases of American development. To its immediate parent, the 'organizational society,' Consciousness III owes not only its technological-material base but also its strengthened vision of freedom, individuality, compassion, and cooperation."*)

* Max Ways, "The Real Greening of America: A *Fortune* Editorial," *Fortune*, November, 1970. Reprinted in *The Con III*

Now, if there is no culture worth speaking of to be *against,* the Counterculturists must try to create *the* culture in the same manner in which the culture creates the counterculture. There are many ways to assert *the* culture in order to have a counterculture. A main one is to establish the counterculture by using the same techniques *the* culture does, such as the "rip-off" (stealing —an honorable American institution), or the press conference.

> Everything about a successful press conference must be dramatic, from the announcements and phone calls to the statements themselves. . . . Constantly seek to have every detail of the press conference differ in style as well as content from the conferences of people in power. . . . Remember you are advertising a new way of life to people. Watch TV commercials. See how they are able to convey everything they need to be effective in such a short time and limited space. At the same time you're mocking the shit they are pushing, steal their techniques.*

Books on the counterculture naturally contain analyses of *the* culture, often written at unconscionable length. The most famous Counterculturist production is, of course, *The Greening of America,* by Charles Reich. That it first appeared in the pages of *The New Yorker* says much about the seriousness with which *the* culture takes the counterculture, as well as vice versa.

Reich anatomizes the American corporate state and finds that

Controversy: The Critics Look at "The Greening of America." New York: Pocket Books, 1971, p. 42.
* Abbie Hoffman, *steal this book.* New York: Pirate Editions, 1971, p. 69.

America is one vast, terrifying anti-community. The great organizations . . the apartments and suburbs . . . are equally places of loneliness and alienation. Modern living has obliterated place, locality, and neighborhood, and given us the anonymous separateness of our existence. The family, the most basic social system, has been ruthlessly stripped of its functional essentials. Friendship has been coated over with a layer of impenetrable artificiality as men strive to live roles designed for them. Protocol, competition, hostility, and fear have replaced the warmth of the circle of affection which might sustain man against a hostile universe.*

What strikes you about this analysis is the amount of exaggeration it contains. Just as *the* culture characteristically overstates almost everything, so the Counterculturists also strain to make their points, more or less in imitation. There may be truth to Reich's view of American culture, but the overkill used to demolish the corporate state casts doubt on Reich's major discovery, that a new man with a new consciousness is emerging.

That may be for the best, since a serious counterculture might look like this—an account of a hike with a woman journalist through Germany in 1932:

One Sunday out in the suburbs of Berlin we met a strange troop by chance on the road. . . . They looked like juvenile delinquents, like black-leather-jacket hoods. They had the vicious and tormented expressions of hooligans. They also had the most bizarre headgear: black or grey derby hats of the sort Charlie Chaplin wore, old ladies' hats with the

---

* *The Greening of America.* New York: Bantam Books, 1971, p. 7.

sides decorated with little bunches of feathers and
medals, working-man's caps of the type sailors
wear . . . they had handkerchiefs and scarves of
loud colors tied around their necks, half-nude
torsos emerging from t-shirts frayed away into tat-
ters, arms marked with fantastic or obscene tattoos,
ears loaded with earrings and rings, and leather
shorts topped by big triangular belts, also made of
leather, covered with mystical figures, human pro-
files, inscriptions like "wild and free" and "bandits."

. . . At the head of the group was a big kid with
sensuous lips, and eyes ringed around with
makeup, who carried a banner. This was Winnetou,
the guru of the band.

He was not very talkative. But he said enough
for us to learn that we had before us a wild clique,
a savage band, a gang of disoriented and asocial
adolescents, a commune of kids rejected by the
community.

Two years later, the woman journalist told me
that, after Hitler had come to power, she met in
the streets of Berlin a sinister and powerful Brown
Shirt, the member of a Sturmabteilung. She was
surprised when the Nazi spoke to her familiarly,
even with affection. Finally she recognized him. It
was the guru of the clique she had made friends
with. It was Winnetou.*

---

* from *La Peste Brune* (*The Brown Plague*) by Daniel Guérin.
Reprinted in *Muhammed Speaks,* December 10, 1971, p. 30.

Credentialism (or Lifefill)

About an Opportunity Offered to but Six in Ten Thousand

A life of accomplishment, sufficiently noteworthy to warrant legitimate reference interest, provides an opportunity—and with it a responsibility—to enrich the public record . . . and preserve among family treasures . . . an accurate, verified recording of one's personal public achievements.

The Achiever has this responsibility to fellow citizens of our Democracy, to the impressionable younger Americans so dramatically in need of worthwhile models on which to pattern their lives, to the professions handling the day's news, to writers and researchers, to historians and biographers.

Along with this societal responsibility goes a directly personal duty to one's self and one's family—the duty of maintaining for posterity a record of one's life activities in a form that will assure its availability to those it will interest and benefit.

—solicitation to buy *Who's Who in America*

Do you want to be one of the six in ten thousand who end in *Who's Who in America*? Needless to say, you'll need the right credentials and a *Who's Who* sort of attitude.

Amassing the proper credentials for your journey through life can be a full-time business, and it's wise to start out soon. First comes school. Success in school is not merely a matter of good grades, popularity, high marks for citizenship, the "right" attitude, and the ability to tolerate Shop, Physical Education, or Home Economics without physically assaulting the teacher; you must also *endure* school. Increasingly, education means keeping youths out of the labor market rather than teaching them anything new, useful, or challenging. "Don't drop out," the "Public Service" Pitches repeat (see "Public Service" Pitches); thus, students remain students longer and longer. Since a good proportion of those in college are dullards (those who weren't to start with may have become so through education), courses must be invented that are interesting enough to keep students awake, "relevant" enough to make them feel "involved," and easy enough to let them pass so that they *stay in school*. The trivial and the obvious are elevated to the level of course requirements, and the student is taught that faking it and the real world are interchangeable. A great many fellows in fakery of one sort or another emerge.

Most of those reaching *Who's Who* have graduated from college, and since only a relatively small percentage of Americans are college graduates, your chances of making *Who's Who* are greatly increased by the possession of a bachelor's degree. Next, the job. It takes experience to get a job and a job to get experience. The riddle appears unsolvable, but millions of job applicants have stumbled in desperation on the answer. Experience can be invented. Your experience is presented in your résumé. In a good résumé, fact and fiction blend so nicely that the personnel department cannot separate the two. Of course, prudence demands that previous jobs made up out of whole cloth have been held with defunct corporations or people now dead, but the applicant need not worry overly *if* his résumé sounds convincing. That is the thing about the credential—it must convince, whether a company, a landlord, or even a date.

The credential having obtained the job, the job can be used to obtain other credentials. One type of credential is the credit card. (There are people, you imagine, who collect credit cards as others collect stamps or autographs, the object being to unfurl them impressively from a special wallet, like yachting pennants.) Without a job you can't establish a credit rating and hence will be denied the credit cards. However, effective use of the credit card requires that the job be one that permits deductible business entertainment. To have a credit card and a job in the mail room or secretarial pool is, in a sense, a contradiction in terms. Credentialism thus develops a momentum of its own.

Tax deductions for business reasons, and many other forms of activity, are made much easier through acquisition of the proper title. Any title is better than no title. A title with "executive" in it is always useful. (See Executalk.) "Vice" something or other is good, and so is "chief" ("chief of industrial relations"), "senior" ("senior editor"), or any type of "consultant." "Aide" is better than "assistant," but "assistant" can be made to work if you can get enough punch behind it. "Assistant to the Director of the International Cooperation Administration for Congressional Presentation of the Mutual Security (Foreign Aid) Program" —a real title. "Advisor" is all right, too.

Astute individuals can outflank organizational titles altogether. One way is to call yourself "Dr." or "Prof." even when what you are a Dr. or Prof. in has no bearing on what you do. (Another is to bestow a "Dr." or "Prof." on yourself when you haven't a Ph.D.) Or, find a situation permitting the use of "with" or "of," such as "with" or "of" an "institute" or "institution." Whether it is more advantageous to be "with" or "of," or "with" or "of" an "institute" or "institution" (or even "institutes," as in the National Institutes of Health) is moot. According to former Senator Eugene McCarthy (whose title might also be "Hon."; many former office-holders, though not Senator McCarthy, could equally be titled "Dishon."):

> *Institution* does sound more certain, more permanent, and more absolute than *Institute*. Why Mr. Schultze is "of" and not "with" the [Brookings] Institution raises another question. People are said to be *with* the government; for example, *with* the Department of Agriculture. Mr. Schultze used to be *with* the Bureau of the Budget. He is now "of" the Brookings Institution. The explanation may be theological. Angels, for example, are *of* a particular choir (of the Cherubim or of the Seraphim), not *with* it as a violinist might be said to be *with* the New York Philharmonic.*

But even if the right title has been found (or created), the competition for a listing in *Who's Who* remains keen, and credentials of other kinds must still be sought. Indeed, they may well be essential for those not engaged in business or industry, the two most-traveled roads to *Who's Who*, whose self-classifi-

* "Whither Economic Policy," *Commonweal*, May 19, 1972, p. 262.

cation scheme for those who are under consideration as listees makes no mention of professor, artist, writer, etc., though, perhaps, for reasons of space. One credential worth having is social; it's helpful to be mentioned in a social directory even if you have to agree to buy the book to get in. If authors are not *that* important for *Who's Who,* authorship is, and candidates are advised to appear in print, even if they need a ghost writer to do it. (Don't be ashamed to hire a ghost writer; today, even writers have ghost writers.) Don't forget membership in professional societies, and never mind if the professional society is more interested in membership fees than in qualifications. An opportunity to join a board of directors must never be refused (unless you have a dozen or so directorships already).

Let's assume your career has developed according to plan. There has been accomplishment galore—honorary degrees, memberships, committees, chairmanships. You have become a sponsor of this cause and that and your name has become visible. You wait . . . has your lifetime been in *vain*? Have you kept your nose clean for *nothing*? One day a letter comes. You read "*Who's Who in America*" on the envelope. You open it nervously. "An opportunity offered to but six in ten thousand"—and one of the six is you!

"Culture" Cant

"Culture" (in the sense of the arts) is one of those words like "beverage" or "leisure" which seem attached to an earlier America. The arts are as fragmented as the rest of American society and quite as infused with pretentiousness, mystification, ego-boosting, and commercialism. The matter has reached such a point that when somebody mentions "culture" you think of anthropology or a pearl.

"Culture" means films, paintings, writing, museums, symphony orchestras, and the rest. Culture with a big "C" is always desirable, whether you mean it or not. From a Litton Industries annual report:

> Stained glass is technical as it is artistic. It is a unique combination of creativity and craftsmanship in conveying meaning through symbol, parable and allegory from one age to the next. Furthermore, the unity of design from a diversity of shapes and colors suggests an organizational form also respected by Litton:
> A flexibility of management in bringing together a diversity of talents into a meaningful whole.
> As we see more clearly how the free economy works, and as we come to understand what makes

it so productive, we are learning how to challenge
human abilities more and more fully.*

But business should not be blamed for "Culture"
Cant; the commodores of conglomeration (who have
replaced the captains of industry) are only imitating
the cant of "Culture" itself. Take the following quotations, which have been picked more or less at random
from an endless assortment of similar confections:

PAINTING TO BE WORN

Cut out jackets or dress from acquired paintings,
such as Da Vinci, Raphael, De Kooning. You may
wear the painted side in or out.
You may make underwears with them as well.

1962 summer†

*   *   *

I must paint of the emotions of space;
describe the charged nothingness,
the volatile and emotional galvanism between
                                    here and there,
the visual energy of space.
The observer must feel with the fingertips of
                                    his eyeballs
through beyond the canvas.
It is the journey of my communion with paint.

*   *   *

Helen Frankenthaler continues to work in the
crisis area of freedom and necessity: more and

---

* I asked a writer of many annual reports whether he took them
seriously. He said, "Are you crazy? Nobody who writes annual
reports takes them seriously."
† Yoko Ono, *Grapefruit*. New York: Simon and Schuster, 1964,
1970, 1971, unpaginated.

more, internecine war flares where reason and un-reason dance their padded knife-fight. She paints our case: how to be intelligently free under the Cheshire-cat smirk of self-consciousness. This is deadly pressure: in this show "problems" seem to have been summoned, under the guise of "images," to ease it. In most cases this takes the form of a bled or aggravated square or rectangle which serves as the domicile shaken by the return of the prodigal chaos. *Black with Shadow* is one of the pictures that try for unity through the biology of painting rather than, like Newman, through its physics. Perhaps it demonstrates the savagery that obtains between the two: the black square braces against the kiss of an orange leech, while a waste of eggs and energy spumes from the jarred rigidity. This is an embattled artist.*

Etc.

It's hard to disagree with George Balanchine:

> I don't read the critics. Even if they don't like a ballet, it doesn't make any difference. We still do it and we have a full house—whether the critics like it or not. It's the public who decides. They see it and say, I like this or I don't. On Broadway, it's different. It's *so* commercial. And the tickets are *so* expensive. The producers don't give a damn about art—only money. If the public doesn't go, they close the show.†

with Andrew Sarris, film critic of *The Village Voice*:

> Film critics have a responsibility to the industry; it's okay to pan, but you can't *dismiss* a movie out

* Quoted in Ralph Colin, "Fakes and Frauds in the Art World," *Art in America*, No. 2, 1963.
† "Work in Progress, George Balanchine" (interview), *Intellectual Digest*, June, 1972, p. 7.

of hand. There's this sense of propriety with the investment. Criticism, therefore, is a form of exploitation, though less so if you're writing for small-circulation journals.

People say they want to see serious things, but they don't. Public taste is awful. The critic has a choice—to cater to it or fight. It's hard to fight. You don't make the choice consciously, but to get this mammoth public off its ass, and to keep the movie business alive, you resort eventually to hyperbole. The critic develops a vested interest in getting people to see things. If they don't he'll have nothing to review. As a film critic I want them to go to the movies, even though the idea of judges' deciding what's good and what's bad is nonsense.

At least, though, we're less corrupt than literary critics, because they want to write whereas we have no ambition in movie making. Literary critics are like one novel reviewing another.*

with Stephen Weil, Administrator of the Whitney Museum:

At its worst, the cant in the art world is unspeakable. It foists on the American middle class the idea of art for a European aristocracy. The first European museums were palaces captured by the people from the aristocracy, and this palace feeling has uncritically been adopted and continued by some American museums. There is still the show-off spending of huge amounts of money for a painting. The fake solemnity and fake seriousness of museums—and the conference rooms designed to make trustees feel powerful—are all part of the attempt to seem aristocratic. Why can't we do something else to make people feel good other than to make them feel like second-class dukes? The same operates in, say, music. Why does the

* Interview.

orchestra wear tails? Because it's what servants wore.

Many younger artists resist the notion of art as a commodity and deliberately make things that can't be carried away. Art, they insist (quoting Lenin), belongs to the people, and yet, come to think of it, why should it? More cant. Too many of the people who come to museums can tick us off their schedule and say they've paid their cultural dues. The future of art museums is filled with questions.*

or with the editors of the *Mediterranean Review:*

There is a great deal of self-hypnotic intoxication with the words going on at present—particularly of the marketable sort we find in, say, Sandra Hochman's *Walking Papers*—which generates a milky, passionless effusion. Such writing may be a symptom of our culture, but it lacks an aesthetic, and it lacks the pitiless objectivity with which a writer must explore not only his culture, but his own experience.

For all the attention to "Culture," where is the "Culture" that escapes dollars and sentimentalizing? Beauty may be skin deep, but ugliness goes to the bone.

---

* Interview.

Deus Ex Computer

Deus ex Computer (God from the Computer) is a new version of *deus ex machina*, an element that appears, in a play or story, suddenly, as if out of thin air, and makes possible the seemingly impossible—providing a *solution*.

Deus ex Computer solutions naturally involve the computer. There are, I know, terrible arguments between the crisis apocalyptics, who say the computer is taking over, and the computer people at IBM, whose answer is "All you have to do is pull the plug." (Of course, maybe you can't get to it in time—what with the computer sending out force fields and rays.) But apart from disputations *about* the computer, there is a way of using the computer *in* disputation, by simply invoking the computer. You might say, for instance, "I think this is true," but it's much more convincing to announce that the *computer* says so.

A simple version of the technique is shown by income-tax accountants who send tax returns to a computer center to be tabulated, the theory being that the IRS will be so impressed by the *computer* that it won't question the figures that were used. Astrology ads like "Let the Computer Teach You About Yourself and What the Future Holds for You" are similar in spirit:

the computer adds authority. Computer logic is held to be unassailable (better than human), and the answers on the computer print-out seem hard to argue with. But he who puts the computer in the role of God can be seriously suspected of trying to play God himself. (See Hyperrationality and Pseudo Infallibility.)

Double-Bind Abstractions

"The Manhandlers. Campbell's soup is one of them."
In this mumbo-gumbo, the nonsense word "manhandler" serves for a class of things that can be made into soup. But what is a "manhandler"? It isn't soup. This is a motivational-research appeal to housewives to want to "handle" Hungry Man. Another example: the *Chicago Tribune*'s slogan, "An American Paper for Americans." What is an "American" paper?

Aristotle, who made the first compilation of formal fallacies, would have classed Double-Bind Abstractions under the category "Affirming the Consequent." In the classical version, Affirming the Consequent occurs when two terms are assumed to be interchangeable but actually aren't. The spectacular advance in our day is to give reality to something that isn't real and then interchange it with something that is—for instance, when people are described in terms of other people who are actors with conscious acting styles, as in "an Arthur Treacher butler figure." The result is complete confusion about who's playing roles and who isn't. A TV producer wants to portray cops and robbers and looks for actors who resemble cops and robbers. But the cops and robbers have been watching television. *They* try to act as cops and robbers do on the screen.

Double-Bind Abstractions finally cast doubt on whether there *is* a reality. Reality becomes image—as when a woman observing a beach picnic said, "It looks just like a vodka ad."

Empathetic Fallacy

When feeling is subtracted from meaning, the Empathetic Fallacy can result. A fallacy, of course, is something that seems to be right but isn't, and the pathetic fallacy is the mistake of believing that inanimate objects have feelings like human beings. The Empathetic Fallacy is the mistake of believing that humans *lack* feeling, as inanimate objects do.

The Empathetic Fallacy appears to stem from a distrust of feelings (your feelings or those of others). There may be a fear of pain or a worry about not seeming businesslike, military, or scientific enough. The result is a way of speaking and thinking about things in which the emotion has been eliminated—a major reason why an idea can sound interesting when presented orally but when the originator puts it on paper the juice is gone. Suppose you feel the present approach to welfare recipients is too impersonal and cold, and you have a better way. Everybody likes it when you explain it, but then you write it up as 'a proposal for the Department of Health, Education and Welfare. A rhetorical chill-factor is added:

ICE ASSOCIATES

A new organization founded by a team of senior research personnel with dedication to social change and concerned with improving the quality of urban life.

Purpose: The goal of Ice Associates is to coordinate the high motivation found in existing action programs with systematic problem-solving and problem-defining methodologies in the social sciences, in order to restructure them to optimize maximum communications possibilities through changing the role of definitions of the participants in the program.

Belief: Too long have social-action operations and decision-makers in general in their quest for objectivity been characterized by a feeling-gap between the spheres of emotion and action. Operations and research must now be combined to ensure that the program is reality-based and subject to continued assessment as to the efficacy of communications.

Hence: Ice Associates proposes to re-form as the Ice Communications Group.

Here is a real-life example which relies on Executalk:

The *voluntary sector,* as represented by one of its largest *components*—the United Way—is mobilizing its *resources* of money, time and talent in response to the *call to arms* issued by President Nixon in his inaugural address. *New* programs are being established, sources of federal funds are being *tapped* to finance *citizen-planned projects, streamlined techniques* are being adopted and funds are being *reallocated* to spread available money more widely, and *campaign goals* are being set substantially higher. To *single out* only a few examples . . . [Italics added.]

Humbug! This pot of message wants to say that not a nickel or a minute of time is being wasted by do-gooders. The last thing that will be admitted is that the objects of solicitude are human beings. The charity "executives" are almost embarrassed to admit they deal with people. As Carroll E. Izard remarks in *Science:*

> We can ill-afford to reject reason for emotion. But we must accept the place of emotion in individual life and human affairs. We must learn to let emotion play its proper role in the reasoning process. . . . We have been taught the emotions, especially what we call the negative emotions, are dangerous and bad.

As soon as you've lost the feeling of people—as soon as you've swapped individual humanity for statistics, generalizations, abstractions—you are off and running down the road to Vietnam, where you "resettle in place" instead of burning down huts or you "waste" instead of kill. (The odd thing about wasting is that it's socially acceptable. In America, obviously, we waste a lot.)

Executalk

"Daddy," said the six-year-old, waving his father's Executive International Charge Card, "I want to be an executive when I grow up."

Everybody wants to be an executive, just about. Then you get to fly on Executive Flights, stay at Executive Inns, have an "Executive Indemnity Plan," eat "Executive Salami," maybe become a "Chief Executive" or "Boy Scout Executive"— or, if you get fired, style yourself as an "Executive Consultant." Nobody is willing to be a manager, a secretary, or a messenger unless "executive" can be worked into the title.

Executives have a way of sounding brisk, authoritative, efficient. They like catchy phrases like "economic game plan," or "action agenda." You never hear of a "lazy" or "ineffective" executive (though there must be some) but only busy and effective ones. Executives revel in snappy endings, like -ist, -ate, and -ize. When you finalize and eventuate you sound like a machine tool with a sharp, hard edge, which is the way executives are supposed to sound.

The drawback to Executalk (a variety of Image Words) is that often in using them you must speak as though you had a mouthful of roller bearings. It's actually harder to frame a thought with Executalk.

"Name of the game," for "point" or "purpose." "Bottom-line consciousness"—"Does that man have bottom-line consciousness?"—instead of "understanding of profits." "Waste management" for "garbage disposal." Compare "eyeball" with "look at," "authenticate" with "verify," "umbrella solution" with "best answer," "overfly" with "fly over," "formated" with "laid out," "ballpark estimate" with "rough guess."

Question: Why would busy executives take the harder way? Answer: They want to prove that they're "executives." But why should they have to prove it? Possibly because, for all the "know-how," they lack the "know-why."*

Executalk, like some of the other language groups discussed, seems essentially designed to boost egos. For business and professional people, it conveys status and a sense of expertise. It imparts a spirit of individualism to a corporate world where there may be little or none.

---

* "A good many of the special words of business seemed designed more to express the user's dreams than his precise meaning," says William Strunk in *The Elements of Style*.

Fadthink

In this age of volatile convictions and unstable beliefs, we are tyrannized by the transitory. Usually the young get hell for it, but if you look at great metropolitan newspapers carefully you'll find Fadthoughts sprouting like poppies on Turkish hills. Politicians wouldn't be caught dead without Fadthoughts. Professional pols, like L.B.J., can put two Fadthoughts in the same breath: "The only way to deal with population explosion is with the knowledge explosion." Or Ramsey Clark: "Change is the dominant fact of our time." Or the Democratic Policy Council:

> Our humanity is assaulted by inadequate schools, by the crushing costs of available health care, by racial injustice and unequal opportunity, by a crisis in housing and transportation, by the foul air and water which pollute our environment, and by a rising rate of crime.

If everything's a crisis, where's the crisis? Built on Fadthink, issues quickly become repetitious, then exhausted. Politicians run out of speeches, reporters out of stories, peace people out of slogans, demonstrators out of crowds.

According to Charles Silberman in *Fortune:*

The volatility of public opinion is the result of two deepening trends of long duration. One is the widening of individual choice that the diffusion of affluence has produced; the other is an erosion of faith and tradition stemming from the growth of rational, skeptical, scientific modes of thought. The era of fads is apt to last a long time.

That's the optimistic version. The pessimistic one is that there has been an erosion of rational, skeptical, scientific modes of thought and a fracturing of choice, to such an extent that Fadthoughts and Fadcauses replace cohesive philosophies. That, at least, was how it sounded when George McGovern was speaking in a crowded New York ballroom in 1971. It was a Politician's Dream. On the tables were clusters of balloons, nodding sagely. The politician had a bag of rhetorical presents and was handing them out: something for the blacks, the young, the environmentalists, the hard-hats (and hard-curlers), peaceniks, Puerto Ricans, Chicanos, one-lunged miners, Indians, Gay Liberationists—I don't believe he overlooked a single group. On the ceiling were banks of burning lights, and as he was talking the balloons broke loose, and two or three at a time, as the audience stared in fascination, they rose to the ceiling and nestled up to the lights. Finally, some balloons started to explode. "Blacks." *Bang!* "Youth." *Pop!* "Women." *Ssssstt—bang!* "Peace." *Bang! Bang!* "Gay Liberation." *Pop!* "Ecology." *Bang! Pop! Bang! Bang! Bang! Bang!** (See Thermopolitical Rhetoric.)

---

* For a fictional forerunner of this episode, see James Joyce's "Ivy-Day in the Committee Room," in *Dubliners.*

Gutspeak

Gutspeakers speak from the gut, which is to say, from below the mind. Gutspeakers chatter about the forgotten language of touch and feeling, the unification of consciousness and body, of getting back in contact with *being*, with the real *you*. If only they weren't quite so . . . earnest!

> Children by nature are sensitive, involved in sense play and exploration: in-a-sense. Social and formal education stress the cognitive and motor functions of the organism without regard for sensory development. We teach them non-sense. This lack of sensitivity creates desensitization: an imbalance in being; a loss of feeling; senselessness: inhibition-alienation-depression-anxiety-deadness.*

A key Gutspeak word is "joy." By "joy," though, Gutspeakers don't mean a sense of merriment at the awful complexity of life, the appreciation of a flower, the satisfaction of having accomplished something hard, humor, or anything like that. They mean getting down to your guts-glands-gonads, *Expressing Real Feel-*

---

* Bernard Gunther, *Sense Relaxation Below Your Mind*. New York: Macmillan, 1968, p. 20.

ings. Forget about thought. *Get Rid of Guilt* (as if there weren't a place for guilt in the world):

> How is joy attained? A large part of the effort, unfortunately, must go into undoing. Guilt, shame, embarrassment, or fear of punishment, failure, success, retribution—all must be overcome. Obstacles to release must be surmounted. Destructive and blocking behavior, thoughts, and feelings must be altered. Talents and abilities must be developed and trained. It sounds overwhelming, but there is cause for optimism.*

Sliced like an apple, the Gutspeaker is an optimist down to the core. All manner of pomposity, clichés, and irrelevancies are justified by the omnipresent optimism of the Sincere Self:

> Consciousness III starts with self. . . . The first commandment is: thou shalt not do violence to thyself. It is a crime to be alienated from oneself, to be a divided or schizophrenic being, to defer meaning to the future. . . . No one judges anyone else. This is the second commandment. . . . A third commandment is: be wholly honest with others, use no other person as a means.
>   —*The Greening of America*

"No one judges anyone else"—how can we *not* judge others (even their lack of joy)? ". . . be wholly honest with others"—but how? Not to do violence to oneself *ever* implies a self so simple in texture, so narrow in circumference, so monominded in design that no part of it is at war with any other part of it. This is not the sort of self I for one should like to be the self of.

---

* William C. Schutz, *Joy*. New York: Grove Press (paper), 1967. p. 23.

Historical Analogies

Watch out for Historical Analogies. They're a favorite device of policy-makers, and they may be used more to serve the interests of a policy than the interests of history.

Many Historical Analogies can be reduced to what Aristotle called the fallacy of accident which arises from taking an accidental property for an essential one. Take Vietnam again. (A great deal of fakery seems to have come to a head, as it were, as a result of that war.) General Matthew B. Ridgway thought it was a second Korea, and so did General Mark W. Clark, who learned from Korea, "The sure way to maintain the peace is to be strong militarily and unafraid politically, and to let the enemy know that we will use that strength to maintain the security of the United States." Eugene V. Rostow, of the Yale Law School, remembered the Soviet-Finnish conflict before World War II, and claimed that if the United States did not maintain its position of dominance in Southeast Asia it would be reduced to the status of Finland—subject to Russian will. Secretary of State Dean Rusk continually compared Vietnam to Munich—an American withdrawal, he said, would lead to further aggression like Hitler's. Lyndon Johnson himself compared North Vietnam's actions to those of the Japanese at Pearl Harbor and believed that the American actions in Vietnam would be justified on the same grounds as our involvement in World War II. But the superficial resemblance to resisting aggression is accidental to the essential problem—the implications for the United States of a Vietnam civil war. In the case of Vietnam, there may have been *no* good Historical Analogies.

The point is, people often act first and find suitable analogies later.

Hyperbole For Our Team

> We can write new and even greater chapters in
> the history of the business press—and I say we
> must. We must for it is our destiny. The business
> press is the greatest continuing teaching machine
> ever devised by man. It has brought our society
> from horse-drawn cart into the nuclear age, and
> it continues to be needed. In its absence, or by
> its weakness, our whole complex society will be
> bogged.
>
> —E. B. MAST, Fifth Annual Spring
> Management Conference of the
> American Business Press

Hyperbole for Our Team is justified (when its users
recognize it for what it is) as being good for team spirit,
for the cause, or for the human race. Aside from labor
unions and trade associations, the most frequent users of
Hyperbole for Our Team seem to be the people who
want to change things the most—that is, the ideolo-
gists. "[Frantz] Fanon's method," says his biographer,
David Caute, "is to fuse the descriptive and the normative, to put the 'like it is' at the service of 'like it ought
to be.' "*

There is the question of whether confusing the

* *Fanon.* London: Fontana/Collins, 1970, p. 15.

descriptive and normative, changing the "like it is" to bring about the "like it ought to be," doesn't change the "ought to be" when it arrives. This may not matter when the "like it ought to be" seems to be a very far-away proposition. In the United States, though, there is a fine line between present and future, and tactics may have a direct bearing on what the future will become. The classical revolutionary uses hyperbole to rouse the masses out of passivity. In America, hyperbole is used to lull the masses *into* passivity. You get hyperbole for breakfast, lunch, dinner, and bedtime snack. The question is, doesn't hyperbole equal conformity?

Hyperrationality

If somebody accuses you of being "too rational," he
may mean that you are too exacting in your approach
to the world. But he might also mean that what you
are asking is too difficult and even too dangerous. We
disagree on what is too difficult and too dangerous,
and that helps account for disputes over what is "too
rational."

The Hyperrationalist differs somewhat from the
straight rationalist, even a rigorous one, because he is
also a theorist—a "scientific" theorist. For Hyperrationality denotes the overreliance on "scientific" approaches
to "problem-solving." It has to do with what can be
called the "fallacy of scientific method"—drawing a
generalization from an incomplete induction.

Hyperrationalist inductions tend to be incomplete
because they ignore, or minimize, activity that is random, unplanned, unplannable. Contrary evidence, un-
answered questions, alternative explanations, even
authentic facts, are safely stored out of sight by the
Hyperrationalist. By reducing the world to abstractions,
the Hyperrationalist blocks out that which causes inter-
ference, falls short of requirements, or just gets in the
way. The result is a vacuum-sealed, highly structured
view of reality. Hyperrationality may be, then, the

mind-set of the technocrat, the social engineer, and the military analyst.

Hannah Arendt, the political scientist, has written in *Crisis of the Republic*, ". . . much of the modern arsenal of political theory—the game theories and systems analysis, and the scenarios, written for imagined audiences, and the careful enumeration of usually three 'options' [see also Many Points] . . . has its source in this deep-seated aversion [to the accidental]. . . . The fallacy of such thinking begins with forcing the choices into mutually exclusive dilemmas; reality never presents us with anything so neat as premises for logical conclusions."

Now let us consider an approach that is the antithesis of Miss Arendt's, that of Herman Kahn, the military theorist. Kahn wrote:

> Under these conditions [of post-atomic attack], some high percentage of the population is going to be nauseated, and nausea is very catching. If one man vomits, everybody vomits. It would not be surprising if almost everybody vomits. Almost everyone is likely to think he has received too much radiation. Morale may be so affected that many survivors may refuse to participate in constructive activities, but would content themselves with sitting down and waiting to die—some may even become violent and destructive.
>
> However, the situation would be quite different if radiation meters were distributed. Assume now that a man gets sick from a cause other than radiation. Not believing this, his morale begins to drop. You look at his meter and say, "You have received only ten roentgens, why are you vomiting? Pull yourself together and get to work."*

* On *Thermonuclear War*. Princeton: Princeton University Press, 1961, p. 86.

To Kahn, only by being tough-minded can we prepare for a possibly grisly future and ameliorate it as best we can.

The military analysts, from their point of view, are "objective." They take a "given," like the possibility of thermonuclear war, and attempt to analyze it to secure the "optimum" results. Theoreticians like Kahn argue that the danger of nuclear war exists as long as nuclear weapons are in circulation. No military analyst is capable, any more than Miss Arendt is, of eliminating the weapons or ensuring that they are safely stored at the UN. Even if good will prevailed, the possibility of *accidental* nuclear war would still be present, and, once accidental war is admitted into the calculations, a defense posture very much like the one we have emerges—even assuming no nation will ever deliberately attack us. To put this apparatus in place in the safest possible manner requires imagining the future— which means forcing choices, even into mutually exclusive dilemmas. In other words, the dilemma, from a rational point of view, seems absolute, the impasse total, and the possibility of nuclear disarmament remote.

But is this logic objective? It is important to remember what can be called the "science-bias," which assumes that there is a rational body of knowledge called "science" separate and distinct from other kinds of reason, removed from the give-and-take of marketplace activity. Military analysis is thought to be objective because it is "scientific"—that is, detached. But perhaps the military analysts are not as detached as they might seem. Indeed, they have a point of view: in nuclear matters, that the dreadful weapons cannot be dismantled because no possibility of serious disarmament exists. The point of view to a large extent is the acceptance of the *status quo*.

Kahn, therefore, has an intellectual belief: that the *possibility* of nuclear war is inescapable, and this possibility would exist even without fears of Communist aggression. As another respected analyst, Thomas C. Schelling, has written, "whether the weapons be light planes with atomic weapons aboard or clubs, nations will find themselves an armory." This is a position quite as important as "hawk" or "dove." If I say, for instance, that pollution will always be with us, I am likely to put my efforts into water filters and face masks. I am accepting the unacceptable, just as Kahn did in his book title *Thinking the Unthinkable*.* And when the military analysts say that they can face, even bravely, the fact of uncertainty about the possibility of nuclear war, they are also saying that uncertainty in nuclear matters is *certain*. Therefore, the weapons must continue to slumber, erect in their submarines and silos.

But words like "uncertainty" and "accidental" do not represent abstract disembodied conditions, though the analysts seem to treat them this way. There are degrees of uncertainty, just as there are degrees of confidence you can attach to different propositions. "Accidental" is accidental only within the limits of possible accidents; the "parameters," as the systems people say, of "accidental" nuclear war are precisely the dimensions of the existing weapon systems. Working from theory, military analysts make the assumption that accidental war is an acceptable risk because no nuclear-disarmament scheme can eliminate the threat of nuclear warfare altogether.

---

* "Unthinkable," of course, is a contradiction in terms.

Now, the analysts are conspicuous by their avoidance of sentiment ("an attitude, thought, or judgment permeated or prompted by feeling"), as though feeling interfered with good analysis. Their faith is in their brains. "Our reasonings grasp at straws for premises and float on gossamers for deductions," said Alfred North Whitehead; the Hyperrationalists entertain no such modesty about the capacity of the human intellect. We can and we should distinguish between what is narrowly rational and conclusive and what is reasonable given our limitations and the persistent danger. When the reasonable and the rational become enemies—as the Hyperrationalists have almost caused them to become—head for the hills. (See also Big-Timing, Empathetic Fallacy, Imperfect-World Routine, Pseudo Infallibility.)

Image Words

Critics craving to do good through unearthing evil are quick to attack as fakery words that may be moving in the right direction. "Senior Citizens" (as in "Senior Citizens' Thanksgiving Day") is an easy phrase to criticize, but think of the wonders "Senior Citizens" might accomplish if old folks were helped to stand up and demand to be respected. When "maturing" is attacked as a tongue-twister for "middle-aged" it's like hitting some of us in the gut. What does "middle age" *mean*? If youth means appearance, health, energy, sexual vigor, years left to live, today's middle-aged person may be young (and maturing—personally, I'm maturing). When you call a spade a spade, you don't need a club.*

This said, we turn to Image Words. There must be thousands of them, all trying to push through the turnstiles of your mind—like the subway at rush hour. Image Words are *busy* words. They want to do something, or get you to. They'd like to sell a policy, increase sales, move people around, build reputations, make the tough look easy and the undone look done. Image

---

* See, for instance, Grace Hechinger, "The Insidious Pollution of Language," *The Wall Street Journal*, October 27, 1971.

Words are a major reason many feel they live in a hall of mirrors.

But instead of peppering away at random, let us concentrate on a few really bad offenders, one class of whom—no doubt about it—are the real-estaters and developers. They promote things like Golden Age. Golden Age is a different proposition from Senior Citizen. A citizen can be senior, but old age most probably is not golden. It can be golden in a sense to persuade, con, or shove the elderly into "retirement communities" with their "gracious living." To me, "Swingles Village" says "swindle." In the image crucible, "laboratory" comes out "research facility," perhaps in an "industrial park." Apartment buildings are given names like the "Cézanne" and the "Van Gogh" when the halls need paint. Who took the studio out of the "studio apartment"? An ordinary high-rise, with walls you can put a fist through, is a "pavilion," "tower," or "towne house"—upper-class England stands in the American memory like a crenelated castle at Disneyland. The sign in front of a down-at-the-heels housing development is falling, but you can still read ESTATES.

The money game is made to order for Image Words. The money merchants love calling the financial business a "game," but "money" is never used when "funds" can be substituted. "Funds" sounds safer than "money," and it's got more mystique. "Investment" is used instead of "gambling" (even though you're gambling), and if you have any funds left after "profit-taking" from your "blue-chip securities," you can put your quarter into the machine at a "toll plaza."

Psychiatry is a veritable swamp for breeding Image Words like mosquitoes. Here is a group of them redefined:

Inadequacy: an incapacity to perform well in spheres other people think are important

Adequacy: a capacity that someone else has to perform well in spheres which you think are important

Authoritarian: descriptive of the way in which other people stand in your way when you want something

Democratic: descriptive of the way in which other people get out of your way when you want something

Aggression: the overt behavior of people who know what they want

Passivity: the overt behavior of people who do not know what they want and who need psychiatric personnel to inform them

Psychotic: a person who understands his own reality.

Neurotic: a person who thinks your version of his reality is the appropriate one

Reasoning: the ability to take facts and come to the conclusions that other people would have come to even if they had never had access to those same facts in the first place.

Rigid: being set in ways which get in other people's way

Flexible: not being set in your ways because you don't have an idea of what a way is in the first place

Projection: unloading your bad feelings on good people

Displacement: unloading your good feelings on bad people

Paranoid: a logician with a fractured premise

> Patient: a human being who really, just between you and me, is a total loss
>
> Psychiatrist: a man whose profits depend upon the maintenance of total loss
>
> Psychologist: a man who is at a loss defining what is a total loss*

If you have "sacrificed expression to communication . . . what you communicate turns out to be abstract and dry," says Bertrand Russell. But your communications people think "communicate" is the hottest thing in growth words. They take courses in "communications arts" and use a ball-point pen called The Communicator. They change the name of their company to include "communications" and run ads reading "To communicate is the beginning of understanding" (AT&T). Until Image Words came along, "communication" meant "sharing"—but the communications division doesn't want any back talk. It wants to dish it out, not take it, so it "municates" instead. (Cowles Munications?)

The "decision-maker" who clears the vocabulary for the military-industrial-government complex is a genius of Image Words. He not only knows about critics like George Orwell, who said that the political language is increasingly marked by "euphemism, question-begging and sheer verbal cloudiness"; he has interpreted such warnings as blueprints and guidelines for more of the same. Consider such achievements as foreign aid (half of it guns), cost overrun, counterforce, defoliate, Bicentennial Era, forward strategy, allies, countdown, conventional weapons (is killing conventional?), coun-

---

* Earl Rubington, "The Psychiatric Dictionary," *The Subterranean Sociology Newsletter,* Vol. III, No. 1.

tervailing, protective reaction, clear-and-hold, fire-free zone, nation-building, peace dividend, pacification, Vietnamization, spinoff, debrief, Free World. The Army mess has recently been changed to "dining facility."

Image Words often rest on confusion as to meaning, sometimes deliberate. In New York there is a group called "Singles for Creative Politics"—pure image-stuff. Take "progress." "Progress" is an upbeat notion, but people who use it often mean "change," which can be for the worse. Or "knowledge," as in the statement "In our fast-paced world knowledge has doubled in the past twenty years and can be expected to double again in the next twenty." Russell again: "Knowledge is a vague concept . . . because all that we count as knowledge is to a greater or lesser degree uncertain." That there is nothing uncertain about "knowledge" as the word is used at present rests largely on a confusion of "knowledge" with "information," which may well have doubled without necessarily bringing a general rise of "knowledge." Such confusions may often be attributed to the growing habit of using Image Words to enhance status. "Knowledge" is a classier idea than "information."

Image Words can be—and often are—self-protective:

> . . . recent case of female hysteria . . . in New York City . . . a Spanish woman entered a bar to get telephone change. Nobody understood her, she became excited, somebody called the police, she became terrified, the police took her to a hospital, nobody understanding a word, and there she was forcibly held for five days, now in a state of total madness. Only on the fifth day did a social worker visit her tenement home and find

two babies dead from thirst in their cots. That was
what she had been trying to say. She was listed
on the hospital records as a female hysteric.*

  "Terminal illness" is an Image Phrase which might
be applied to the language itself. But the meaning of
"terminal illness" I prefer is getting sick at the railroad
station.

---

* Lisa Hobbs, *Love and Liberation*. New York: McGraw-Hill,
1970, p. 56.

Imperfect-World Routine

Because the world is imperfect, imperfect actions must be taken (and insurance taken out), or so the Imperfect-World Routine has it.

Most of our categories are nonpartisan, but the Imperfect-World Routine is unexceptionably conservative in implication. It is used to defend positions that are attacked as "immoral" or "tough." The defender replies, "But it's an imperfect world," and the moralizer loses the argument.

When the architects of American nuclear defense were criticized for opposing total or partial nuclear disarmament, they said the world was imperfect. For Albert Wohlstetter, "The world, as I've said, is a dangerous place, and I find the idea that war can be eliminated implausible."* To Herman Kahn, "I owe a lot to the classical economists. They were often limited in their considerations, but people like Adam Smith taught me that life consists of hard choices. Economics is often called the dismal science, and for a reason. You never know when the good you are trying to do will cause harm instead. Innocence, in my view, is a major sin. Economics teaches you this, as it teaches

---

* Arthur Herzog, *The War-Peace Establishment.* New York: Harper and Row, 1965, p. 68.

you to look at problems in a detached way. From fairly early in life I wasn't afraid to face hard questions."*

In challenging the Imperfect-World Routine, don't insist on the world's perfectibility. Ask rather if it is not the fundamental assumption of imperfection that itself leads to imperfection. (The "self-fulfilling prophecy.") Ask whether there are less bleak assumptions that can be explored. (See also "Next Demand.")

---

* *Ibid.*, p. 76.

Kid Crap

> I know that you can understand how deeply moved
> I am, and my wife and daughter are, by this won-
> derful reception. You probably wonder what Tricia
> said to me while the very great applause was
> running up through the rafters. She said, "Why,
> Daddy, this is better than our convention in
> Miami." And, of course, my answer was, "Why,
> there is a reason for it. They are young."
> —RICHARD M. NIXON

Everybody who isn't one secretly hates kids. I say
this without the slightest fear of contradiction. Adults
don't like to admit that they hate kids, and often they
praise them overly instead, but down in their bones
they hate them.

The reason is not entirely a matter of jealousy. Kids
are widely hated by adults because, while the adults
are more or less force-fed fakery, the kids accept it
willingly and even try to use it to their own advantage.

Take age. This is the first country in the world where
kids have been given the absolute right to decide what
youth is. The wielders of this awesome power, in
theory at least, could put the boundary of youth at any
age, from thirty-five to seventy-five. The only obstacle
might be the chronological territoriality of other age

groups who insist on equal rights. For instance, Senior Citizens might decide that the Golden Age begins at thirty. That, indeed, would be a logical outcome of the trend. Everybody would be a kid until thirty and then immediately qualify for half-price tickets to the movies.

The kids talk about "human communities" and "human ends," but if you turn your back they take out their portable computers and start calculating how old you are. They pretend to be interested in character and spirit, but all they really want to know is whether you are a kid. If not . . .

Not only is there a tribe of budding market researchers and behavioral psychologists behind the beards and under the beaded headbands, but they're cowards, too. A study by the psychiatrist Leon Eisenberg showed that biological adolescence begins four years earlier than it did only a century and a half ago. An individual is capable of assuming adult roles ever earlier in life, assuming that intellectual and biological maturity have a relation. But you don't find the kids fighting for a voting age of fourteen.

The point is, the kids are in the same condition as everyone else. At the first sign of a recession, they start worrying about careers. At the first disappointment, they give up politics. If they swap mates at the communes, they succumb to jealousy. If they become discouraged, they resort to marijuana instead of tranquilizers. If they have the chance to push their faces on TV, they eagerly take it. If they can stave off working, they do. All this we can accept because we see it in ourselves. It's the *Kid* Crap that makes us hate them.

Many Points

Greek logicians recognized Many Questions as a rhetorical device which was meant to so confuse the opponent that he started to babble. Few ask questions today, but many make points.

Many Points is a sturdy rhetorical trick. It is designed to state the issues in such a many-faceted way that the opposition is reduced to rebuttal and quibbling. It is the debater's version of the old rule that the best defense is a good offense.

Presidents often give three reasons for something. One or two points are too easy to argue with; after four or more, people lose interest. Three is the right number of points for Presidents. Nixon always gave three reasons for the American presence in Vietnam, though it was evident he really had more than three because they weren't always the same three. Americans are in Vietnam, he said once, (A) to defend democracy, (B) to defend the American national interest, and (C) to avoid losing our first war. On another occasion he said:

> A nation cannot remain great if [A] it betrays its allies and [B] lets down its friends. Our defeat and humiliation in South Vietnam, without question, would [C] promote recklessness in the

councils of the great powers who have not yet abandoned their goals of world conquest.

Many Points has the advantage that if several points are wrong, one or two may still withstand scrutiny, though chances are that the same mind which made two mistakes or even one will be mistaken clear through. Thus *Christian Crusade Weekly* argues, "Upon analyzing the philosophy of the sexologists it has become quite clear that the primary purpose of these social engineers are [*sic*] to: (a) discredit Christianity, (b) alienate children from parents, (c) render ineffective the Hebraic-Christian moral code and (d) transform the United States into a new social order." What is the *secondary* purpose of sex education?

Many Points can be freighted with emotional overtones, to add to its impact. "In order to extend the *modern* American *empire* by waging war against the *people* of Vietnam, the government has increasingly moved to repress political opposition at home. Moreover, the physical and cultural destruction of the Vietnamese *people* reflects a much older and deeper *policy* of *physical and cultural destruction* of the Black community at home, and is now being carried into new versions of racism by the Administration in its *betrayal* of civil rights and its aid to *counterinsurgent* police forces in the great cities."* The point may (or may not) be correct; the verbiage undermines possible validity. Many Points is a slipshod device, and arguments that use it tend to collapse under their own weight. When somebody says "various ways," look for excess baggage.

----

* Resolution of the Radical Historians' Conference, 1969. (*Italics* added.)

Mincing Words*

Mincing ("characterized by or expressive of affected daintiness and elegance"—*Webster's Third*) Words are familiar to everyone in their older forms: "powder room," "little girls' room," "gents." Despite greater frankness and more frequent use of "gutter obscenities" in print, film, and theater, Mincing Words are still popular. Most people still prefer "birthday suit" or "stark naked" to "bare." "Nude" is a tepid compromise. "Prurient interest in sex" hints at some more rarefied way of approaching it. "Feminine hygiene" and "dainty" coexist with the scented vaginal douche. The idea behind "premarital intercourse" is that sex leads to "holy wedlock" (or deadlock). Otherwordly language about sex even occurs in otherwise candid books about sex like pasties on a strip-tease dancer. Sometimes, the antiseptic language is deliberately chosen as insurance to discourage charges that the authors have a "prurient interest in sex." (See Sexperts.)

As for profanity, it is still minced out of the public record as ungentlemanly and unscholarly, though few people balk at its use in conversation. Take the fate of "shit." In the spring of 1970, Luciano Berio, the

---

* I am indebted to Laurence Urdang, former editor of the *Random House Dictionary*, for this concept.

composer, having conducted some of his own work at a New York City concert, turned to speak to the audience. Recent events had depressed him and, forgetting the music, he said (or words almost exactly like them), "Every man and country have within them a flower and a piece of shit. Tonight America smells like a piece of shit." The *Times* reported:

> Mr. Berio spoke his mind briefly about Vietnam and the students. . . . The Italian composer said that America has within its soul both flowers and fertilizer, and at this moment we are smelling more of the latter.

That such innocent profanity as "shit" or "bullshit" should be under anathema today appears as one of those minor vanities to which the country is habituated, unimportant alone but stultifying in heavy doses. Norman Mailer's exhibitionistic and quarrelsome campaign slogan for Mayor of New York—"No More Bullshit!"—was systematically blotted or blipped out. Judge Julius J. Hoffman objected strenuously to defendant David Dellinger's characterization of a police officer's testimony as "bullshit." ("Never in half a century have I heard such language in a courtroom.") The *Times* showed its predilection for agriculture as it spoke of Dellinger's "barnyard epithet." *Times* drama critic Clive Barnes said in a review, "I was distressed to find that Odets's original use of the word 'manure!' had been replaced by something more modish and shorter by two letters. . . . It removes the musical from the realm of family entertainment."*

---

* An impressive earlier example of trepidation in the face of "bullshit" was its deletion, at the start of this century, from translations of newly discovered plays by Sophocles. According

The reticence to use the earthy language survives, as if mixing the scatological with the serious destroyed the credibility of the latter. There is hope, though. In the best tradition of fearless journalism, both the Chicago *Daily News* and the Chicago *Sun-Times* used Delinger's "barnyard epithet" in full.

As noted, "shit" and "bullshit" can be easily overworked, but frequently they are indispensable.

---

to Alexander Gross, the suppression had a broader significance than mere good manners. "In an irrational and almost religious way, [scholars] have tried to foreclose the entire question of the identity of the Greeks as the founders of Western culture. The deeper one pursues Greek mythology and the possible nature of many of the plays, the less 'Western' they begin to appear, and it is perhaps understandable that scholars have closed their minds to what must have seemed to them dangerously close to Oriental abandon or even (heaven forbid!) primitive African rites." *New American Review*, No. 5, January, 1969, p. 137.

Newsthink

Newsthink* is the rhetorical bias of the news media in favor of news. Perhaps no other fact today concerning information is more important—and more neglected. The vested interest *of* news *in* news being what it is, news will not easily admit to creating news. It is too busy announcing it's NEWS.

This is one thing you never read in texts on journalism or in rueful reminiscences by the grizzled sages of the profession. When the news is attacked, it's for being slanted in some direction or other, as in the well-remembered foray against journalism by Vice President Agnew, who thought the news was unfair to the government. In fact, the news *was* slanted, in Agnew's favor. It gave him space. As an interested party, he could not ask what the real news bias is.

So the thing to worry about in news is not so much whether the story is *the* story but whether it's *a* story. Some of the ways of making stories look like stories are so elementary that nobody even thinks about them—such as putting headlines, date lines, and by-

---

* Not to be confused with George Orwell's "newspeak," which was a recasting of the language for totalitarian purposes. "Newsthink" or "Newsspeak" serves other purposes.

lines on them; indeed, such as running the story in the first place. But a story is not a rose.

Take some of the words of the poets at the news desk, the headline writers: "assail," "attack," "accuse," "hit," "denounce," "berate," and their cousins from the controversy factory. You don't just *make a comment or two* about the village master plan, you don't even *dissent* a little. What you do is assail it. At least, the headline writer and the reporter say you assail it, even though all you did was remove your glasses, wipe them with a handkerchief, and demur. Your "opponent"— as he is called—does not just comment on your comment: he assails *you*. It looks like news, but the story is really happening down at the news desk.

Another device of Newsthink is to build in errors. Errors are usually blamed on bad reporting, haste, misquotation, poor information, and other hazards of the profession, but, after all, errors may make news where accuracy won't. Errors can be *advantageous*. A misquotation may be better than no quotation. Or suppose a couple of punks are trading shots. It isn't much, but call it a "shoot-out" and you've got the makings of a story. Or a "riot." Only three people, technically, are needed for a riot; call it a riot even when a trio is "rioting" and there's a slot for the story on the front page. It is often the same with the statistics on crime or drugs. It may be better *not* to check them out too closely. ". . . The system of reporting ensures that errors of fact and interpretation may be repeated, compounded, and reformulated as myths," says Max Singer. A central reason is that reporters want to be on the front page, and another that there must *be* a front page.

Tagging, trending, and countertrending are some other tested methods of Newsthink. Tagging consists of putting an identifying label on someone and then proceeding to always identify him by the label. The label itself is chosen in unconscious concert by the Fourth Estate for being newsworthy. George McGovern, for instance, got tagged as a mackerel—a colorless fish with a large mouth—and for this reason wasn't given a chance to win the Democratic nomination. Lyndon Johnson's label read POWER MAD, Bobby Kennedy's RUTHLESS, and Gene McCarthy's LAZY and COOL. If the person so identified manages, through sheer genius, to assert some other side of his personality, which had been there all along, the news then says he has "changed" or "matured." He's ready for a new label.

What we may call trending occurs when the news media decide on a trend, such as the "law-and-order" trend. All the information on the subject will then reinforce the idea of the trend. A good example is the youth trend. In 1967 the youth trend was away from politics; in 1968 into politics; in 1969 out of politics; in 1970 back again, then gone again, like some incredibly indecisive mass-minded Enoch Arden. The Cambodian incursion got the youth out in full fury, but before you knew it they had vanished back into the woods. They were registering in droves for the eighteen-year-old vote, but then again they weren't, just as they could be expected to be a decisive influence in the future, except that they wouldn't vote, until they suddenly reappeared in the McGovern campaign, and then failed to vote.

Countertrending is based on the journalistic tradition about a man biting a dog. The general idea is that if the public has a perception about what is happening, one sure way to make news is to work against the perception, which trending may have established in the first place. Say the country is gradually moving left.

There might be a story in saying it's going right. As soon as everyone believes there is a strong drift to the right, countertrending calls for saying it's moving left again. News can make news by contradicting *itself*.

Another way news makes news is to heighten some of the reality and forget the rest of it. What emerges is a clear-cut event when what really happened wasn't clear-cut at all. Words like "leadership," "operation," "timetable," "plans," "concerted," and so on are like molds into which reality is poured. Making news also means the effective use of "news makers." A news maker is one who always gets space no matter how banal his utterance. News makers, for their part, are well aware that because reporters want their by-line on the front page, it is relatively simple to utilize them. At the same time, the news maker must be careful. He can't be sure how the reporter will handle the story and how it will look in print. Rarely do news makers tell the whole truth.

The point is, journalism needs *stories*, stories that conform to Newsthink's definition of what's news. The dogmas of the news business about news—"timely," centered on news makers, careful when it comes to "vested interests" and advertisers—help guarantee that trivia will be produced by the minute or the column inch. A detailed survey of the major news media demonstrates that they virtually ignored for years such stories as pollution, smoking and cancer, population growth, auto safety, and hunger in America.* One story never

* Robert Cirino, *Don't Blame the People*. New York: Vintage, 1971. The main news outlets examined were *The New York Times*, the *Los Angeles Times*, the Honolulu *Star-Bulletin*, Walter Cronkite, and "The Huntley-Brinkley Report." They were studied over various periods in the 1950's and 1960's. The author comments: "Spiro Agnew's claim of a liberal bias is

covered is how much the news media cater to the attitudes of their owners; Newsthink holds that news tries to be "fair," ignoring completely the question of bias.

Because of the idea of what news *is*, the news produced is often guaranteed to be out of date before it is reported. And what is reported is all too likely to be unreliable. If news were considered as something broader, less subject to "breaking" stories and the requirements of time, if a certain skepticism were applied by newsmen themselves as to what is *news*, that *would* be news.*

---

contradicted by all the major studies of bias conducted during the last thirty years. That the people were not shocked by Agnew's accusation is itself testimony to the fact that for over thirty years the media have been using their power to spread corporate propaganda, protect the establishment from unfavorable news, and prevent true competition among ideas. The subsequent popular support for Agnew's position is a function of media's intentional failure to communicate the most basic ideal of a democracy—that all ideas, popular or unpopular, should be given a chance to compete fairly for public acceptance." (p. 5.)

* A nondogmatic newspaper might handle news in a totally different way—without "stories," so to speak, at all. It might look at almost nothing but "breaking trends."

Next Demand (Precedent Pap)

The Next Demand principle (which could also be called Precedent Pap) is phrased as "If I give you this, next you'll demand that. Since *that* is unacceptable, I won't give you *this*." The argument is used extensively to rationalize the *status quo*.

Next Demand refutations can be heard in arguments against the legalization of marijuana—"The next thing they'll want is heroin"—or against proposals for a guaranteed national income—"Next thing, they'll want socialism." The Next Demand principle was sounded by Vice President Agnew in connection with the Attica prison riot: "A Governor of a state cannot allow himself to be peremptorily summoned into the presence of out-laws to meet their demands. Had he gone, and still re-fused to surrender the state, the next demand might have been for the President of the United States to demean himself in their presence."

The fallacy of the Next Demand rests on the failure to make a distinction between what is irresistible and what is not. If by assenting to the present demand you are bound to accede to the next one, there may be good reason for saying no. But when you can say "no" to the next demand even if the present demand is assented to, then conjuring up the Next Demand is a rhetorical trick. The President could have said no even if Governor Rockefeller had gone to Attica. Besides, going might have been the right thing to do.

Nonsense

Nonsense: something that's minus sense, conveys the absence of sence, non-*sense*, as in "genuine leatherette," "natural Naugahyde," "medium premium gasoline." ("Frankly Fake Fur" is not nonsense, however.) "The sound of a half-truth is the hardest to discern. Often it seems to go bonk for a while. But sooner or later it plinks. People, companies and governments forget this." (From an advertisement.)

There is a kind of nonsense that isn't really nonsense, it's just phrased that way: "Matched stereo speakers which are unmatched." "Receive Occasional papers regularly" (Center for the Study of Democratic Institutions). There is also the partisan nonsense we have all come to accept: "I'm not embarrassed to be George McGovern's seventh choice for Vice President," said Sargent Shriver. "We Democrats may be short of money. We're not short of talent. Think of the comparison and then you can pity poor Mr. Nixon—his first and only choice was Spiro Agnew."

When it comes to nonsense, though, Mr. Nixon is not to be outdone. Take the following illuminating exchange. Said the Reverend Dr. Abraham K. Akaka, in a sermon delivered in Honolulu:

We can show people that on God's ukulele no string says to any other, "You don't belong" or "You must look and sound like me." In a one-string ukulele or a ukulele whose strings all have the same sound, such a ukulele would be terrible. Also each string must find its right pitch and that right pitch comes from the tuner, from God. No string can say, "I don't need God, I will set my own pitch." See what that does to the world.

Answered President Nixon:

It was worth coming all the way to Hawaii just to hear this service. I have never heard a sermon that was more eloquent, more appropriate, and timely not only for this event, this day, but for this period in the history of the world.

Nonsense, however, is not restricted to ceremonial occasions. It may well spill over into actual policy. Peer deeply into the following.

The Shadow of Mao Tse-tung can be seen and felt in the United States today. We can expect the subversive danger to grow as time passes. The only way to meet it is to be prepared. This the F.B.I. is doing through its investigations and the training of its personnel. For example, we are giving instruction to F.B.I. agents in the various Chinese dialects. In this way, our agents are capable of conversing in the native tongue, and the F.B.I. will be able to handle present and likely future contingencies.

—J. EDGAR HOOVER, 1970

Now let us look at some more nonsense.

Oneness

Oneness (an appeal to mass naïveté, like Candor Con) has it that we are all *one*, down deep. One nation indivisible, one people, brothers and sisters under the skin, Americans all, arms linked, we march into the sunset toward a common destiny.

Be wary of the B.S. Factor when you hear exhortations to Oneness, as in "my fellow Americans," "the corporate family," "togetherness," "community," "neighbors." An example of plain old Yankee commercialism being palmed off as neighborliness:

> *Gratefully* acknowledged are the *generous public-spirited* business *neighbors* who make possible this *friendly call of greetings* from your Welcome Wagon *Hostess* on behalf of the *civic, religious, cultural* and *social service organizations* of the *community*.
>
> —Welcome Wagon (Italics added.)

"Civic-minded," "community spirit," "neighborly," "friendly," "religious"—arf! Often it seems that the only things the community will rally around are the Little League and the zoning laws. Mrs. Beatrice Munro at least was frank when she declared: "My father, Henry Lounsbury, zoned Bedford, New York, for four-acre zoning in 1921. I have fought to keep it four-acre zoning and I will fight for it until I die."

When the blacks or the lettuce pickers call for One-ness among themselves, they have a specific set of group objectives in mind. Similarly, the American women's-rights movement calls for Oneness among the "sisters"—although, for my money, Women's Lib ig-nores the fact that "women" is not a discrete category, since women are also heterogeneous mem-bers of different classes and groups, with different interests in terms of roles, income, political persuasion and so on. This may indicate that Women's Lib can proceed only a certain distance before serious differ-ences in objectives emerge, if they haven't already. But the trouble with Oneness as often used is that the real purpose is partisan—that is, to achieve the aims of some or a few, as when the "corporate family" is men-tioned when wage increases come up, or each of the two parties sanctifies the two-party system, meaning that each of the existing parties remains intact.

When Presidents invoke Oneness, speak of "we" (meaning "them" and "us"), bewail "divisiveness," and so on, they may want to find support for their policies, yet they also try to submerge the differences that do exist. Better, perhaps, to affirm the divisions, and try to solve them (through adversary proceedings if neces-sary) than to declare a state of unity which is largely imaginary, causing shock waves when the real differ-ences emerge, as they always will.

Placebos

In medicine, a placebo is an inert substance given for its psychological effect—to satisfy the patient—but there are other kinds of placebos:

> The Human Development Institute, a subsidiary of Bell and Howell, devised a ["sensitivity"] training kit for the National Alliance of Businessmen and is now also trying to peddle it to poverty groups. The kit contains material to help managers deal with poor black people in a more understanding way. For example, there are black and white masks. In one skit a black masked man plays he is coming to work late. He is confronted by his supervisor who is wearing a white mask. In this way, white employees get to feel what it is like to be a black man.
> —as reported in *Hard Times*

That's nice. When the white employee learns to feel what it's like to be a black man, maybe he'll just conclude he's glad to be colored white. *Consumer Reports* offers another kind of placebo, month after month evaluating products but failing to consider whether a product is so trivial as not to be worth an evaluation. Common Cause, at least in its literature, hands out placebos like candy. "Don't just sit there and complain—Let's do something to rebuild America." Well and good, you guess, but what? C.C. thunders about closing tax loopholes and limiting campaign spending, but do such nostrums "give the country back to the people," as Common Cause demands?

The people-placebo, the participation-placebo, the power-placebo—they seem to be manufactured in the same place as campaign placards, by a dolt with a stencil. I, for one, am not entirely sure who the people are; I know I'm supposed to help give the country back to them, but to which people? The people should wear badges to identify themselves. . . . Many, though, seem genuinely pleased at being people, which allows them to "participate." People are commanded to participate, made to feel guilty if they don't—slackers of democracy, enemies of the people, to the guillotine! Participation is taken as an end in itself. Don't ask, "Participate to what end?" Just participate. And that is how the world will end, with half the people participating and the other half arresting them for it.

If special licenses were required to distribute placebos, politicians would have to have them—and not just the old guard. The populists, who demand power to the neighborhoods and community control, would need them too. Ex-Senator Fred Harris, for instance, espouses "people control over government services in their own communities." Big cities like New York could be "divided into communities which elect their own Mayor and Community Boards . . ." which could then tax, spend, and run their own schools, fire and police departments, sanitation . . . One result (aside from endless disputes as to which community a fire is burning in or where the garbage is to be dumped) would be more politics, and more placebos.

Placebos relate to Problem Problems.

Problem Problems

A Problem Problem arises when something is identified as *the* problem when it is not the problem or is only part of the problem. Problem Problems generate more problems than existed before.

There are various kinds of Problem Problems. One is blaming a false problem instead of the real problem. Thus, the hard-hats took it out on the long-hairs wearing peace medallions as though they were responsible for inflation, unemployment, and other things. President Nixon resorted to the Problem Problem when he blamed the Soviet Union for the failure of his plan to end the war in Vietnam. The Black Panthers were held responsible for provoking incidents with the police, but

> the chilling fact remains that in 1968 and 1969, nineteen black young men identified as Black Panthers were shot and killed in Chicago, Los Angeles, San Diego, Long Beach, Seattle and New Haven. Four policemen were killed during the same period in gunfights with the Black Panthers in Oakland, Santa Ana and Chicago. It is significant to note that according to the Lemberg Center at Brandeis University, "of 381 racial disorders occurring between January and August, 1969, only 17 involved Black Panthers and of those 17 only eight were violent confrontations between police

and Black Panthers." Under our system of justice which we ask and demand that all Americans respect, we have the strange circumstance that, almost without exception, where the killing of a Black Panther is at the hands of a police official, the matter has been ruled "justifiable homicide" by a coroner's jury (which is not a judicial tribunal) and the determination of the question "was this killing necessary?" is never brought before the courts to meet the test of fundamental fairness in the administration of our laws.*

Some Problem Problems seem more or less invented, for grants, consultant fees, reputations, or royalties. One test of the reality of a problem is whether, simply, it continues to be a problem or whether, after its debut, it is never heard of again. Foundations, you suspect, deal heavily in Problem Problems, to judge from the fact that many projects listed in foundation annual reports do not reappear in subsequent annual reports. ("The annual reports of foundations are among the most self-seeking documents in American life," says Dr. Orville G. Brim, Jr., former director of the Russell Sage Foundation.) What ever happened to the "invisible government" of the CIA?

Mostly, though, the problem of Problem Problems is a solution problem. People have answers and try to shape the problem to match the answers they already have. According to a Brookings Institution report, discouragement with the major new federal programs of the 1960's brought cries for tighter federal regulation, program coordination, decentralization, greater spending, all aimed at quick results and none achieving them.

---

* "Minorities and the Law," Speech by Charles E. Smith, Judge for the Superior Court of Washington State for King County, April 16, 1970.

> Giving up the search for solutions to urgent social problems would be both irresponsible and dangerous, but taking refuge in pat, simple answers—decentralize, regulate, coordinate, spend more, spend less—seems unlikely to lead to a workable new strategy. It is time for a new and more realistic look at the federal government and the ways in which it can hope to carry out its activities effectively.*

The *real* problem, though, is that people who demand pap will get it. Few in a position to know will say what they think, with the result that rarely, if ever, is it pointed out that there may be *no* answers, or at least no easy ones.

---

* Charles L. Schultze, Edward R. Fried, Alice M. Rivlin, Nancy H. Teeters, *Setting National Priorities: The 1973 Budget.* Washington, D.C.; The Brookings Institution, 1972, p. 455.

Prosperity Put-On

Because the country is rich, many Americans think they have a share of the pie. Poor bachelors with rich girl friends have similar delusions. Seeing the chauffeur, maid, butler, town house, and the rest, they feel rich themselves, boast to others about it, and spend too much money. When the romance ends (money usually finishes it), the rich girl has her town house and the bachelor is back in his "studio apartment" with his memories.

The Prosperity Put-On has two elements: that Americans have the highest standard of living in the world, and that free enterprise is responsible.

> Today the American way of life provides the highest standard of living ever enjoyed by any people in the world. This is no mere boast. [But it *is* a boast.] It is a statement of thrilling fact—that men can raise their level of living by greater productivity if they are free to do so.
>
> —business advertisement

That free enterprise is responsible has been a credo shared by both major parties.

> The American free enterprise system is one of the great achievements of the human mind and

spirit. It has developed by a combination of the energetic efforts of working men and women, bold private initiative, the profit motive and wise public policy, until now it is the productive model of mankind.

—Democratic Platform, 1964

With the rapid economic rise of Western Europe, Japan, and the Soviet Union, the message has been toned down but not altered. Nixon's former Commerce Secretary, Maurice Stans: "Here at last is the economic system that has given men everything that they need, and proved its ability to give them everything that they want." (See Undistributed Outlook.)

The enthusiastic reception the Prosperity Put-On receives is an odd combination of avarice and gullibility. Both can be detected in the propaganda of the New York Stock Exchange ("people's capitalism") or in the daily market reports. Again, the word is optimism. A rising market "spurts," "jumps," "leaps," "bounds." A market that is just milling around, maybe dangerously, is "resting," "pausing," "consolidating" (which means that it is getting ready to climb or "test the 900 level"). Only with reluctance do the financial columnists confess that the market might be heading down. It "retreats" or has a "blue Monday" or is in a period of "tax selling" or "profit-taking." It takes a fairly steep drop to get beyond "dip" or "correction." (See Image Words.)

The same expectations (or dreams) that reinforce the language of optimism can also cause confusion as to what is represented by capital, salaries, and wages. Capital, intelligently invested, is hard to lose, and even though the stock market has not, at this writing, actually reached its 1965–66 level (markedly so if inflation is counted in), there is evidence that a great many rich people have have gotten a great deal richer in the period. Salaries can be lost, and easily—as the recent recession showed. Even pension plans are vulnerable, since usually they can't be taken to a new job.

The soft underbelly of salaries, as opposed to the protection offered by capital, is disguised by the fact that salaries sound somehow more secure than wages. The whole panoply of titles, secretaries, private offices, and expense accounts bucks up the look of the "executive's" security. Should he have any doubts about it, he can remind himself that he is not a "blue-collar" worker. (Unlike him, the blue-collar worker has a union.)

As for the ordinary person, the Prosperity Put-On seduces him with the size of the Gross National Product. (There are, the Canadian Pierre Berton tells us, "alternate standards of living based on scales that do not exclusively chart the consumption of goods and services."*) More than a trillion, and going up, on the GNP computer at the Department of Commerce. It sounds good, until you realize how *gross* the GNP is, including wasted effort, duplication of services, accident repair, etc. GNP-itis reinforces the prevailing notion about American riches, even when symphony orchestras, museums, and educational institutions close for lack of money, even when men in the United States have a lower life expectancy than men in eighteen other countries, when thirteen countries have a lower infant mortality than we do, when women in eleven countries have a better chance of living through child-

---

* *The Smug Minority.* Toronto/Montreal: McClelland and Stewart, 1967, p. 25.

birth than women in the United States.* We need a *fine* national product rather than a gross one.

Another question is how the GNP is divided. The middle- and lower-middle-income groups continue to pay a disproportionate share of the taxes because the Prosperity siren has lulled them to sleep. Few seem aware of the concentration of wealth, much less seek even a modest redistribution of it. And yet—with houses, cars, furniture, and so forth bought on mortgages and credit—what do most Americans really own? The skillful use of the Prosperity Put-On may have made Americans among the most propagandized people in the world.

Nor do the bravos over our prosperity take into consideration how much we must pay for what prosperity we have. Professor Norman Birnbaum says, "the heightened productivity of the system may give rise to a generalized status anxiety in the society, with unpleasant consequences for the transmission of high culture, with a degradation of values in monetary or careerist common denominators, and with feelings of extreme resentment on the part of those who do not fare well in the status competition. If these are the effects of affluence, it is difficult to see why they should be described as 'revolutionary' when they seem to reproduce at a 'higher' level the inanities, crudities, and horrors of early capitalism."†

---

* Cirino, *op. cit.*, p. 113.
† *Social Policy*, July–August, 1970, p. 5.

Pseudo Infallibility

Fame, money, respect, passing marks and prizes, a seat among the powerful or on the stock exchange—many incentives spur you on toward being right; not just humbly right, but 100 per cent, right-on *right*. High on the list of imperatives for being right is the undesirability of being wrong. Few are willing to concede they might be wrong, and fewer confess to mistakes in public. By those in authority, error is seen as mortal weakness and is almost never admitted at all.

Still, the dread possibility of wrongness lingers. When two or more people offer sharply conflicting answers to the same question, one or more is usually wrong. Indeed, all parties concerned may be wrong. Fortunately, wrongness need not be feared if you have mastered Pseudo Infallibility, the art of seeming right.

Clouding the issues in general through the adroit use of the Fake Factor (as discussed in this book) is, of course, indispensable. If nothing else, fakery by definition makes error harder to detect. Pseudo Infallibility, however, is more narrowly defined. It has to do with the proper deployment of experts who use a special brand of fact which can be called the Fact Fact.

A Fact Fact is a fact that seems to stand by itself even when there is no factual evidence behind it. It is made into a "fact"—instead of something more tentative, like "idea," "feeling," "hunch"—simply by assertion of its factuality. If, for instance, I say that there are forty billion roaches in Chicago, and you can't count the roaches yourself, you must sullenly assume (probably wrongly) that somebody has counted them. "At least 80 per cent of feminists are not Lesbians," said Rita LaPorte, National President of the Daughters of Bilitis, a Lesbian organization—and while Ms. LaPorte is probably right, you must wonder, if you're to be objective about it, who's counting. One source says, "Although no current studies are available, we estimate that 30 to 50 per cent of the population occasionally use four-letter words." Little basis, it seems, exists for this and estimations of similar kinds. Besides, the mathematically minded reader will ask himself whether 50 or 70 per cent of the population use four-letter words *frequently*.

Another way to be Pseudoinfallible is to place a Fact Fact in the future, making it a Future Fact. Future Facts (and Future Theories) make ideal tools because they are irrefutable at the moment of utterance (the future not yet having happened) and because when enough time has passed to permit Future Facts to be checked against actual outcomes, nobody bothers to single out the perpetrators of Future Facts that did not come to be. "It isn't the Revolution that faces America but the beginnings of an atomizing civil war," commented columnist Max Lerner oracularly (May 2, 1970). Did "future shock" exist before (or long after) the book? Many experts predicted, in August, 1969, an immediate sharp rise in the stock-market averages. The averages went down. What ever happened to the fearfully awaited doctor shortage? There is shortly to be a glut of M.D.'s, it seems. The continued use of Future Facts which fail to materialize has gone a great distance toward undermining public confidence.

Fact (and Future) Facts which seem a bit shaky can be shored up by repetition. That this is a favorite device of dictators has not deterred its use in a democracy. President Nixon resorted to the technique when he cited the 1954 massacre of hundreds of thousands of anti-Communists in North Vietnam as a reason for American actions on behalf of South Vietnam. If we left, he said, there would be another "bloodbath." Even when this Northern massacre had been refuted, the President, instead of backing off or even qualifying, merely repeated his "facts."* (American military operations,

---

* "On each of Mr. Nixon's two earlier assertions of this historical hobgoblin, I wrote that the record disclosed no evidence that such an atrocity had occurred. Prof. George McT. Kahin, Director of Cornell University's Southeast Asia program, used this space on Dec. 6, 1969, to refute the President's Nov. 3 statement. Several magazine articles have gone into the matter in detail, as have numerous books, each concluding there was no bloodbath in North Vietnam in 1954. . . . the Diem Government itself reported 48,200 arrests of Communists from 1954 to 1960 . . . So the only events resembling mass political reprisal after the 1954 armistice occurred in the South, not the North. What did happen in North Vietnam was a harshly repressed peasant revolt in 1955 and 1956 against a severe land reform program. It had nothing to do with Ho Chi Minh's takeover. Mr. Kahin thinks perhaps 10,000 to 15,000 may have died."—Tom Wicker, *The New York Times*, May 12, 1970. Also, Wicker wrote in a letter to those answering his column of May 12, the suppression of the revolt was "a reprehensible episode, as I have written. It can certainly be argued that it resulted from the process of imposing Communism on North Vietnam. Nevertheless, it was *not* a political reprisal; the process could only be repeated in South Vietnam if that nation were totally in the hands of Communists who wanted to repeat it; and the facts that the land reform in North Vietnam was rescinded, was publicly discredited by the government itself, and is historically accounted one of the gravest errors of Ho Chi

however, were not construed as causing a bloodbath. See Undistributed Outlook.)

In the search for ways to sound infallible, the polls must not be ignored. A Poll Fact becomes a fact by having appeared in print, as when a magazine palms off a poll to show that it has a higher pass-around factor or a greater readership in barbershops than its competitors; politicians produce Poll Facts to prove the public likes them best. The drawback to Poll Facts is that your rivals may also resort to them, as happened in 1969 when all three candidates for Mayor of New York presented Poll Facts proving themselves ahead.*

Fact Facts in general always sound more authoritative when used by the experts. The experts know the techniques: to stay, when possible, on both sides of an issue (a sure way to be infallible), to keep talking until the question period is over, or even, as in testimony before Congress, to use "talking papers." ("The House Armed Services Committee prepares scripts for its side called 'talking papers.' Even generals use them during testimony. They open a drawer and peek," says Ernest Fitzgerald, the Department of Defense official who was

---

Minh, one that almost tore his party and country apart, argue that no such repetition need necessarily be expected in South Vietnam in the event of a negotiated settlement of the war (or even a Communist military victory)." And what about *South* Vietnamese reprisals against the Vietcong when the war was over?

* How political polls are rigged is explained by John Lorenz, a polling expert: "It's easy to load a poll. You can take it in areas where the candidate is strong, or, because people don't usually finish questionnaires, make sure they are finished in the right areas and throw the rest out. Another way is to take a previous encouraging poll and confine yourself to a sample of that sample. Polls often mislead, and there is need for control on the survey business."

fired for revealing data on "cost overruns.") Any kind of expert will do, but scientific experts are certainly best.

Virtually everyone defers to persons of superior competence in a given field; as Robert A. Dahl points out, the technological "expert may be no more gifted than you or I, but by dint of study, training, and experience he knows more about a particular subject than we do." So far, so good. But the *blind* faith accorded to scientific experts can be used handily in pursuit of Pseudo Infallibility.

Science is thought to be infallible because scientists conduct experiments and offer proofs.* Inside the scientific establishment, of course, scientists disagree on everything, proofs or no, and especially about science, but they too try to look infallible. The scientist wants to prove his disinterestedness, his veracity, the inevitable nature of his conclusions, but he does not shout at you—far from it. Everything in his presentation is carefully couched to demonstrate how objective and detached he is. If he does not publish his paper he may not have his contract renewed, but his modesty goes a long way toward making you accept his claims. According to a scientist, J. M. Ziman:

> A scientific paper is . . . a cunningly contrived piece of rhetoric. It has only one purpose; it must persuade the reader of the veracity of the observer, his disinterestedness, his logical infallibility, and the complete necessity of his conclusions. . . .

---

* "One of the unfortunate things about 'facts' that are recorded in scientific journals is that once they have appeared in print it is difficult to eliminate them and they are quoted again and again for many years." Ross E. Hutchins, *Insects,* Englewood Cliffs, N.J.: Prentice-Hall, Inc., 1966, p. 72.

> [Scientists] favor the passive voice, the impersonal
> gender, and the latinized circumlocution, because
> these [permit them to make] relatively positive
> assertions in a tentative tone. . . . This sort of
> shyness is not just a trick for escaping when one
> turns out to be wrong; it is a device of "inverted
> rhetoric" by which an apparently modest and dis-
> interested tone enhances the acceptability of one's
> utterances.*

To seem infallible, then, you want the scientific expert on your team, with his papers, statistics, Flow
Charts, Time-Frame Overlays, Alternative Perceptions,
Division Subsystems, and Final Reports. Often, merely
the presence of an expert is enough to discourage the
opposition. With the right experts to back you up, you
are bound to look infallible and can proceed with im-
punity, as when the U.S. Army boldly disposed of a
nerve gas which, it declared the experts said, could be
safely stored in canisters.

The gas leaked. With the backing of experts, the
Army stored the gas canisters in concrete blocks. Hard
to contain as Dracula, the gas escaped. "We relied on
experts," explained the Under Secretary of the Army,
Thaddeus R. Beal. With the backing of still other experts the gas was dumped into the Atlantic Ocean,
where, said the Army with complete assurance, it would
be perfectly safe. You pray the Army is infallible this
time, but you can't help wondering whether, without
Pseudo Infallibility in the picture, the gas would have
been manufactured in the first place.

---

* *Nature*, October 25, 1969.

"Public Service" Pitches

An especially slippery use of the Fake Factor is what goes on in the name of "public service," a term I take to mean not-for-profit or governmental activity meant to serve the public at large. (In a real sense, the public *is* at large.)

Government "Public Service" Pitches are exemplified by ads to buy United States Saving Bonds (these bonds offered no inflationary hedges and were hardly a good investment) or appeals to contribute to Radio Free Europe. The latter was particularly disreputable advertising, since RFE was not looking for money—the CIA and later other Federal funding provided most of that —but pretending it had broad-based support. It is clear, in fact, that free "Public Service" advertising like this often represents the viewpoint not of the public but of groups with special axes to sharpen. "If NATO wasn't there you wouldn't be there either." Along with the grammar, the logic is poor; it is far from clear that without NATO I wouldn't be exactly where I am. But the point is that this ad, and dozens like it, pretend that particular policy positions are shared by everybody. "Worship at the church of your choice," since it is "Public Service" advertising in space donated by public facilities, says inherently that support of organized religion is state policy. (There is a real question, I would think, as to whether such ads are constitutional.)

The positional schizophrenia behind many government "Public Service" Pitches can be easily seen. "Jury service supports law and order and the American way of life." Is it the American way of life that women and countless others are exempt from jury service in various states? Take two ads across the aisle of the subway or bus. One urges young men to join the military since the skills acquired will guarantee good jobs. The other pleads with businessmen to hire veterans who cannot find employment. That the first ad must have been written with full knowledge of the conditions behind the second (at least for a time, Vietnam vets had the highest unemployment rate of any group in the country) is indication enough that somewhere somebody in authority doesn't "give a damn."

Although the space for "public service" ads is provided free or at low cost, the pitches themselves are obviously written by professional, paid-for copywriters, using all the usual tricks, "public service" or no. "Don't drop out" gives "dropouts" a bad name and implies, despite contrary evidence, that if the potential dropout stayed in school he would do as well as his contemporaries. Many such ads are written in a style so supercilious and condescending (if not positively insulting) that it is almost certain to undermine their credibility with those they are intended to reach.

A NEW OFFER TO THE JUNKIES OF NEW YORK

You know as well as your own arm that you have to rob. And when you rob you may kill. You've got yourself an expensive habit. New York State

has a special division to get you out of this fix.
Dial . . . It's a better connection than the one
you've got.

The "Public Service" Pitch sounds no different from
the ones aimed by the private philanthropies, and these
charities too, in theory, function for the public good.

There is no better guide to the infiltration of the Fake
Factor into charity (that fakery *gets* into charity is indication enough of how pervasive it really is) than the
Spring, 1972, "Wise Giving Bulletin" of the National
Information Bureau. (As we have often noted, nothing
is as it seems. The only kind of information the NIB
issues is about charities.)

HOW DOES A THOUGHTFUL CONTRIBUTOR GIVE WISELY IN 1972?

The answer is not easy. . . .

Contributions go to philanthropic organizations,
not "causes," and like all human institutions in
our society, they range in quality from excellent
to deplorable. . . .

It may prove to be a mistake, however, to base
one's selection on surface criteria. For example:

1. *Old-Line Voluntary Agencies*—It is not possible to assume with assurance that old-line voluntary agencies—the reliable standbys of our parents'
days—are serving effectively priority needs in our
society today. Some voluntary organizations that
started with high ideals have become so *institution-
minded* that the initial goal of service has been
drowned by the organization's desire for self-per-
petuation and self-aggrandizement. . . .

2. *Dramatic Fund-Raising Appeals* are not an
adequate measure of a voluntary organization's
need. The image of a trained dog guiding a blind
man is so appealing that one prominent organiza-

tion providing dog guides still has an unspent reserve of $20,000,000 in contributed funds. (Following public exposure of its finances, the agency stopped further fund-raising some years ago.)

3. *Letterheads Filled with Big Names*—One cannot judge the quality of a philanthropic organization today by the Big Names on its letterhead. Big Names have become a dime a dozen in philanthropy today. Some prominent Board members serve with genuine responsibility and devotion; others, perhaps suffering from an excessive appetite for public attention, welcome listing on as many prominent letterheads as possible, but do not meet even the elementary responsibilities of trusteeship or sponsorship. To illustrate, a national organization with a Big Name Board and over $20,000,000 in annual contributions still has as its paid President a man who posed to contributors as a volunteer for more than five years while receiving a salary of nearly $50,000 a year, an expense account of up to $22,000 a year, and fees indirectly through the law firm of which he was a senior partner. A responsible Board could not have tolerated such an attitude.

4. *Printed Annual Reports* should help in an analysis of an agency's finances and program, and some do. But the picture they give may also be misleading for fund raising purposes. One multi-million dollar national philanthropy reported to the general public in its printed annual report last year that it had in effect a deficit of about $300,000 for the year whereas examination of its audit report revealed it had in fact a surplus of nearly $1,400,000. (Following public exposure, this agency agreed to reform.)

Another difficult problem in wise giving grows out of the changing relationship of voluntary philanthropy to government. Government has expanded expenditures very rapidly in such fields as health, welfare, education, etc., in recent years, but at times has accepted responsibilities which it has dismally failed to meet. Thus public welfare, the last refuge of the desperately poor, is so badly designed and operated that many children and aged persons still suffer malnutrition in a country embarrassed by its annual food surpluses.

When it is discovered periodically that a business boom does not improve the condition of many of the desperately poor (who may just become relatively poorer), political leaders launch at times crusades such as the recent "War on Poverty," as if Washington could resolve by slogans and intermittent splurges of tax funds serious maladjustments in the fabric of our society and severe handicaps in the employment qualifications of many of our poor.

Where can the voluntary contributor's dollar be applied effectively to cure such a situation? We suspect that a solution will not be achieved until the majority of our contributor-taxpayer-voters can be helped to free themselves from the stultifying effect of the myths surrounding poverty and public welfare, myths which have blocked for years adequate voluntary and governmental remedies. To illustrate, jobs will not solve the problems of most of the 13,000,000 human beings dependent in whole or in part on public welfare because:

0.9%	Less than 1% of welfare recipients recently were able-bodied men
55.5%	were children
25.0%	were aged, blind and disabled
18.6%	were mothers with children (about 14% of these mothers were working but earned too little to support fully both themselves and their children).

100.0%

Question: Does not voluntary philanthropy, with its billions of annual contacts with the contributor-taxpayer-voter, have a more important role than it currently fills in relation to this area of basic human need in America?

In the field of health, which cost the American people an estimated 75 billion dollars in the year 1970–1971, governments provided an estimated 28.4 billion, an increase of 3.5 billion dollars in a single year. Of the combined governmental-voluntary subsidy dollar, government provided an estimated 92 cents. In such a situation, what should be the priority functions of the national "health" agencies?

For both the fields of health and welfare, John H. McMahon has suggested that the "hall-marks of *voluntary* effort," above routine basic standards, should be: "indignation, imagination, idealism, and persistence: indignation at needless suffering, imagination to solve problems, the idealism that insists things can be changed for the better, and the persistence to keep plugging ahead until change is achieved."

Quote Facts

Many people appear to believe that because something is quoted it is necessarily true. A Quote Fact is not itself a fact but someone's opinion which becomes a fact or datum by virtue of having been quoted. If I say X, it is no more than Opinion X. If I quote Y on X, it may still be Opinion X but, because I have quoted it, it takes on the authority of Fact X, which is a different matter. Quotations may be valuable as opinions, but where they are conveyed as facts, as arguments from authority, they become another use of the Fake Factor.

The Reverend Billy Graham is convinced that too much sex is detrimental to religion and "mental health." There is little mileage for Graham in merely making this assertion—he needs drama and documentation. Both can be provided by Quote Facts. To the library he orders his researcher, who emerges with the inevitable sociologist quote and something better, a real jewel (if it is not read too carefully), from a theologian who might be thought to disagree with Graham on everything.

> We of the Western World, on a sex binge never before equalled in modern times, should be wise enough to heed history's lessons. For history con-

clusively teaches that the decay of a nation in-
evitably follows the decay of its sex standards.
Theologian Paul Tillich, in his book *Morality and
Beyond,* stated flatly: "Without the immanence of
the moral imperative, both culture and religion
disintegrate." And sociologist Pitirim Sorokin has
warned that "the group that tolerates sexual anarchy is endangering its very survival." (*Reader's
Digest*)

Politicians treasure the Quote Fact, which can be
used instead of research and has the added feature of
permitting identification with national heroes; Lincoln
quotes, whether they pertain or not, are much treas-
ured. Reporters prize Quote Facts for much the same
reasons: they save research, add an extra dimension,
and get the reporter off the hook. Many people who
have had experience with reporters, though, are fearful: reporters misquote you with amazing frequency.

Without Quotesmanship, the ordinary academic or
polemical paper could not be written. Evidently, the
quotations say, "Look how much I've read":

Language is a Janus and will revenge itself on
those who abuse it. "Twenty years' worth of
Americans were taught that to lie was the highest
morality," wrote Andrew Kopkind in *The New
Statesman* for February 24, 1967. Today we can
push Orwell's observations a stage further. If you
spell it backward, it spells Nature's; or, in LBJ's
similarly tail-clutching formulation, "We will continue fighting in Vietnam until the violence stops."
Humpty Dumpty's question about words was what
the French call *exact*—"which is to be the master—that's all." When we come to the euphemisms
of contemporary war politics, when we read of
incendigel and *megadeaths,* we remember Durk-

heim's warning in *Les Formes élémentaires de la vie réligieuse:* "One comes to the remarkable conclusion that *images of the totem creature are more sacred than the totem creature itself.*" One recalls that MacArthur would not lower a flag from an American position in the Pacific although that flag, which was being used as a marker by raiding Japanese planes, was costing many lives daily. This is Swift's Academy of Lagado in reverse.*

Quote Facts can be easily abused. They can be bought and paid for, as in breathless praise for stew or cereal. They can be made to sound informative when nothing of substance is conveyed (" 'Agnew may be right. I don't know,' John B. Kinzle conceded as he tinkered beneath the hood of a car in his service station"—*The New York Times*). They can be used out of context (observe that Tillich can be counted in Graham's camp only if "moral imperative" is assumed to pertain to sex). Generally, the popularity of Quote Facts may indicate a broader truth: when people sound knowledgeable, others believe them. So much in modern life is guesswork and confusion that almost anybody who seems to know what he is talking about will be promptly smuggled between quotation marks.

---

* Geoffrey Wagner, "The Language of Politics," *Language in America*, edited by Neil Postman, Charles Weingartner, and Terence P. Morgan. New York: Pegasus, 1969, p. 33.

Scispeak

Scispeak (a variety of Image Words) tries to invoke the authority and infallibility of science in order to impress you that what is being presented is "scientific"— that is, proved, resting on experiment, based on serious testing, etc. Science means "scientific method," which is inductive, skeptical, and open to doubt, but Scispeak is out to convince and therefore, though it sounds scientific, is really a species of rhetoric.

You can hear Scispeak in phrases like "Science tells us" or "Doctors know." Medical Scispeak, or Physpeak (Physicianspeak), is especially likely to contain false claims. Watch out when you hear the phrase "medical science." A sure sign of Scispeak is the use of long, factual-sounding terminology when simple words would clearly do, as when TV weathermen talk about "fifty per cent chance of precipitation" instead of fifty-fifty chance of "rain."

Each branch of science and social science, no doubt, has its own speak. Let us dwell on just a few. There is Teachspeech, or educational jargon, which includes "manipulative skills" (doing something with your hands) and "continuing education" (or "adult education"). "Syspeak," or systems language, has a heavy input of computerese: "systems," "feedback," "feedforward," "information transfer" ("the application of assimilated data"), "probabilistic," and so on. Socspeak, or sociologese, has words like "achievement-oriented," "peer group," "process."

Jargon may clearly be necessary for specialists at work. It may even be a way for social scientists to avoid making those dreaded "value judgments." It becomes Scispeak when it no longer has any professional necessity or when no specific body of meaning is attached to it but it is used to overcome opposing ideas or bewilder laymen (as scientists use it) or by one layman to impress or fool another or to get a grant.

Thanks to Scispeak, a great cluster of once technical or at least precise words have lost the edge of meaning to the point where they are almost as interchangeable as marbles. Take a three-digit number and find the corresponding words in the table below. Number 343, for instance, produces "intuitive sociometric contingency." Number 914 yields "interdependent power gradient." Soon you will be speaking like a sociologist.*

	COLUMN 1		COLUMN 2		COLUMN 3
0.	evaluative	0.	coalition	0.	equilibrium
1.	functional	1.	power	1.	relation
2.	hyperbolic	2.	influence	2.	attribution
3.	intuitive	3.	communication	3.	contingency
4.	interactive	4.	sociometric	4.	gradient
5.	reciprocal	5.	role	5.	structure
6.	negative	6.	activity	6.	decision
7.	operational	7.	task	7.	network
8.	centralized	8.	status	8.	matrix
9.	interdependent	9.	interpersonal	9.	index

* From "The Systematic Group Phrase Projector," *The Subterranean Sociology Newsletter*, Vol. III, No. 1, p. 13, which in turn was adapted from an article in *Newsweek*.

Sexperts

The American businessman has discovered the vagina and it's like the next thing going. What happened is that the businessman ran out of parts of the body. We had headaches for a while but we took care of them. The armpit had its moment of glory, and the toes, with their athlete's foot, they had the spotlight, too. We went through wrinkles, we went through diets. Taking skin off, putting skin on. We went through the stomach with acid indigestion and we conquered hemorrhoids. So the businessman sat back and said "What's left?" And some smart guy said, "The vagina." We've now zeroed in on it. And this is just the beginning. Today the vagina, tomorrow the world. I mean, there are going to be all sorts of things for the vagina: vitamins, pep pills, flavored douches like Cupid's Quiver (raspberry, orange, jasmine, and champagne).

—Jerry Della Femina,
*From Those Wonderful Folks
Who Gave You Pearl Harbor*

The American businessman is not the only one who has discovered the vagina. So have the Sexperts, who have discovered the penis, too. (Actually, today's penis is full of envy at all the attention the vagina receives.) Sexpertise can be profitable, but you can't just go

and hang out a shingle as a Sexpert—at least, not yet.
You need a degree (preferably an M.D., though a Ph.D.
will do), a large supply of willing informants, a catchy
vocabulary, and an idea for a book. You'd better not,
though, begin to dream about the royalties until the
proper title is found. The early Sexperts, like Krafft-
Ebing, Freud, or Theodore Reik, didn't suffer from the
condition known as titlitis. Their titles said what they
meant without being provocative or cutesy-wootsy (*Of
Love and Lust*). Is, ah, Freud's Krafft Ebing? Ponder
*Any Woman Can!, The Incompatibility of Men and
Women and How to Overcome It, The New Sexual
Fulfillment, Everything You Always Wanted to Know
About Sex But Were Afraid to Ask, The Love Treat-
ment, Group Sex*, and *The Groupsex Tapes*. You might
think that these and literally dozens of others would
have exhausted the imaginations of the hot writer-edi-
tor teams, but that's only because you haven't encoun-
tered *Beyond Group Sex*, or even *Total Sex*.

Sexperts usually begin with the premise—stated or
unstated—that society has screwed up sex. The reason
why the sex books are placed on the PSYCHOLOGY instead of SOCIOLOGY shelves at the bookstores, it seems,
is that the Sexperts say you have the potential (assuming the sex books don't turn you off for life) to have all
the orgasms you can possibly muster if only you learn
to let go: "According to many behavioral scientists,
the healthy, well-functioning human being uses only
4 to 10 per cent of his potential," says one sex manual.*
Such statements are laden with doubt. Despite what
"behavioral scientists may (or may not) conjecture, to

---

* Dr. Herbert A. Otto and Roberta Otto, *Total Sex*. New York:
Peter H. Wyden, 1972, p. 1.

validate the 4 or 10 per cent you would have to find a human being who had "used" 90 or 100 per cent of his "potential." It might be safer to class human sexual potential as a large unknown, rather than conjure up a Garden of Eden where people have orgasms with more or less the effort required to order a hamburger at McDonald's.

Be that as it may, something is wrong, and few seem shy about letting the Sexperts in on it.

A remarkable study was reported by John A. Blazer on "Married Virgins—A Study of Unconsummated Marriages" (*Journal of Marriage and the Family*, 26 (1964), 213–214). Even more surprising to the uninitiated is the fact that this is a follow-up on an earlier study by Leonard J. Friedman (*Virgin Wives—A Study of Unconsummated Marriages*, Springfield, Ill.: Charles C. Thomas, 1962). Dr. Blazer managed to obtain a sample of one thousand Caucasian females who were married but still virgins, the average length of marriage being eight years (mean). The reported reasons these women gave for their continued virginity included: (1) Fear of pain in the initial intercourse (20.3%); (2) Disgust of sex which was seen as *nasty* or *wicked* (17.8%); (3) Impotent husbands (11.7%); (4) Fear of pregnancy or childbirth (10.2%); (5) Small size of the vagina (8.2%); (6) Ignorance of the exact location of their organs (5.2%); (7) Preference for a female partner (5.2%); (8) Extreme dislike for the penis (4.6%); (9) Intense dislike for intercourse without pregnancy (3.9%); (10) Dislike of contraceptives (3.3%); (11) Belief that submission implies inferiority (3.1%); (12) General dislike of men (3%); (13) Desire to "mother" their husbands only (1.4%); (14) Fear of damaging the husband's penis (1.2%); and (15) Fear of semen (.9%).*

Just how people can be so repressed on the one hand and, on the other, be perfectly willing to divulge all the details has never been explained. In any case, Sexperts have no difficulty getting confessions, which they piece together in books. Those quoted are never identified by their last names; you must take it on faith that Judy, Jim, Nina, Nick, Loraine, Bill, Rhoda, Dick, and the rest of the copulatory crew did what the Sexperts say they did.

> . . . a man who reported difficulty in touching his own semen began a deconditioning program by playfully handling warmed yogurt, tapioca, and jello. He then did some fingerpainting and mud-play. All this time his partner helped him with praise, encouragement and support. "I finally touched my semen for the first time and I didn't even shudder. Joan really was great by talking to me when I needed it. The payoff was that I am a lot less careful in bed and out. Much more relaxed and less tense."†

* * *

ALAN: I wonder . . . how many women I've taken to bed in twenty years of swinging.

INT.:   (Smiling) *Can you come up with an approximate figure?*

ALAN: I may need a computer. . . . It comes to . . . 3500 for the first seven years.

INT.:   (After a pause) *What about the last thirteen years—how can we average that out?*

---

* *The Subterranean Sociologist Newsletter*, Vol. 1, No. 1, p. 6.
† *Total Sex*, p. 28.

ALAN: Would you settle for that same fifty week
         average? . . .

INT.:   (Scribbling) *Well, I come up with a total of
         around 8700 women in twenty years.* . . .

ALAN: (Shakes his head rather soberly, seeming
         more shocked than elated about the dis-
         closure) Really, that many?

INT.:   *What's the matter?*

ALAN: (He is scratching his chin now, his lean
         body slouches forward, his legs spread out
         loosely) I don't know. It sort of makes me
         feel, well . . . old.*

* * *

"It was an easy adjustment for us to make," Rob
said. *"You see, Emily and I are brother and sister
in addition to being husband and wife, and once
you've gotten past traditional morality enough to
accept that, it's no big deal to go into swinging."*†

The cardinal rule of the Sexperts is not to seem las-
civious—playful maybe, but prurient never. Sexperts
are not pornographers. Several techniques can be isolated for sounding detached and scientific while discussing an orgy, say. A Sexpert can introduce, early on,
his "sample" or "research population"—"Ninety-three
per cent of our sample were upper-middle-class white
people. Eighty per cent lived in two-family houses.
Fifty-one per cent had dishwashers. The average re-
spondent . . ." This makes his approach sound truly
scientific.

Another device is to use language which, while not
forbiddingly technical, manages to sound authoritative

---

* Herbert F. Margolis and Paul M. Ruberstein, *The Groupsex
Tapes.* New York: David McKay, 1971, pp. 18–19.
† John Warren Wells, *Beyond Group Sex: The New Sexual
Life-Styles.* New York: Dell, 1972, p. 150.

and specialized—"holistic sex," "primal love," "hidden sensory starvation," "sensory concert," "pleasuring," "Orgasm Central Control," "reprosex" (reproductive sex, as opposed to "funsex"), "erotic input," "sexual swindler," "postlude," "Total Pleasure Immersion" (TPI), "Orgasmic Impairment" (OI). You can peruse sex manual after sex manual and never encounter slang like "screw." The Sexpert can counsel therapeutic games, which make it sound as though you're playing house, like the Doll Game, the Genital Mirror Game, or the Goose-Pimple Game. One game, for instance, is to encourage you to make up your own sex talk.

The following are examples of the private sexual vocabulary developed by a number of couples:

Intercourse	Male Sex Organs	Female Sex Organs
nuki-nuki	trouser mouse	jelly box
dinging around	joy	flower
tickle your fancy	gratsel	fratsel
joyride	sunup	rosebud*

Little wonder that the more serious-minded Sexperts fall over backward not to sound like kissing cousins of the popularizers. Masters and Johnson's sex clinic, the Reproductive Biology Research Foundation, is as covertly titled as a secret government military installation, and their prose stands guard over sexual activity like a duenna. ("Voluntary contraction of the external rectal sphincter together with the gluteal musculature may be employed during both the excitement and plateau phases of sexual response. Many women use this stimulative technique when driving for sex tension increment.") Serious Sexperts must sound responsible

* *Total Sex*, p. 76.

in order to fend off those who think the only appropriate place for sex (and sex education) is a pay toilet. Who could argue with the Sex Information and Education Council of the United States (SIECUS), which believes that

> a major breakthrough is necessary to create healthy attitudes towards sexuality. SIECUS believes that man's sexuality is a positive force in his life, and his total well-being depends on the responsible use he makes of this force.

Many people have doubtless been helped by sex education and therapy. The question is whether the "new sexuality" won't be as troublesome in its own way as the old. For one thing, the many Sexperts make sex (and a lot of it) almost mandatory—it almost sounds as though THOU SHALT HAVE INTERCOURSE had been graven on one of Moses' tablets. There is something very mass-minded about the idea that everyone *must* have orgasms: bigger and better orgasms with a big "O," as though on an assembly line.

The stress placed on the Big O leads to a new-style myth: that women have a greater sexual capacity than men. The notion of women's superior sexual capacity is based on the finding that some women can have as many as fifty orgasms in a single sexual session—which makes everybody who doesn't have, or fails to produce in his partner, fifty O's feel absolutely *awful*. Fifty O's! Pity the poor woman who has only a couple of O's or no O's at all. Soon, such a woman will have to wear a scarlet numeral. . . . The equation of sexual capacity with the ability to have multiple orgasms is playing with loaded dice.

Leaving aside any question of morality, mass-produced, impersonalized, even semipublic sex is almost bound to be vulgar in the deepest sense. My candidate for the vulgarity medal among the Sexperts happens to be the most famous one of all, Dr. David Reuben, author of *Everything You Always Wanted to Know About Sex But Were Afraid to Ask* and *Any Woman Can!**

In his preoccupation with quantity, size, and gadgetry, Reuben is as American as the Department of Defense. "The average man pumps about eighteen quarts of seminal fluid in his lifetime" (*Everything*, p. 9). What's average? How does he know?

> The average erect penis sizes out at six inches. The range extends from four and a half to eight inches. The unofficial world record is held by a man whose erect organ was fourteen inches long and three inches in diameter. No information is available concerning where this contest was held [p. 19].

* * *

> Through the wonders of Japanese engineering it is now possible for virtually any man to engage in sexual intercourse regardless of impotence. In spite of its effectiveness, for some reason it hasn't caught on. The device is simple and fool-proof. There is a small black box about the size of a transistor radio with two wires, each attached to an electrode. One electrode is fastened to the base of the penis; the other (specially designed) is inserted into the rectum. When the current is turned on, high-frequency impulses surge through the nerves controlling the sexual reflexes, produc-

---

* New York: David McKay, 1971.

ing an immediate, powerful erection. As long as the power is on, the power is in [pp. 20–21].

Husband-hunting females, Dr. Reuben has the answer for you.

> If a woman can establish herself as the *provider of milk* she literally makes herself part of her man's unconscious mind. Even more important, she is unlikely to be displaced by any other female competitor. Nice legs, a good figure, bright conversation, feminine flattery, can turn the head of most men, but not the one whose woman supplies milk and love in abundance.
>
> On every occasion they are together she must provide him with milk (or the symbolic equivalent) in some form. If they go out on a date, after he brings her home, she can invite him in for hot chocolate or coffee *with cream*. It's even better if she floats whipped cream on top of either drink. If he has his favorite brand of "milk"—that is, beer or wine, she should serve it *just the way he likes it*. (After all, that's the way Mother served her beverage.) Ice cream is a fine substitute, and the most effective ice cream is that made with her own hands—in one of those little crank freezers. Remember, Mother made all the milk herself—or at least baby thought so [*Any Woman Can!*, pp. 242–43].

There you have it, the winning combination: orgasms and milk. I raise my glass of milk and toast the day when all of us from California to New York, in a vast simultaneous climax (time differences notwithstanding), can have our Big O's at once.

Simplex Complex

A sufferer from the Simplex Complex can be identified by his predeliction for finding simple answers to complex questions, which causes him to commit the fallacy of exclusive linearity (uncritical attempts to bring everything under one principle or category), the *reductio ad absurdum,* and other grievous errors.

The Simplex soul of the conservative ilk displays a special fascination with the past, probably because it's easier in hindsight to erase what doesn't conform to his point of view. You can hear Simplex folk of the right talking about the "old verities" as if they were always verities or the "conventional wisdom" with no sense that perhaps it's a contradiction in terms. Chronic oversimplifiers have every look of having ceased to develop, or even function, at some specific moment in time. They are constantly resurrecting the same hoary solutions, accusing the same old bad guys, intoning the same old slogans, and continuing to fight the same old wars.

A PLAN TO WIN—AND SAVE LIVES

General MacArthur told Bob Considine his plan at a birthday interview. Here are the words:

"Of all the campaigns of my life—20 major ones to be exact—the one I felt most sure of was the one I was deprived of waging." The general then outlined an operation that would "have won the war in Korea in a maximum of 10 days. The enemy's air would first have been taken out. I would have dropped between 30 and 50 tactical atomic bombs on his air bases and other depots in . . . Manchuria. Dropped under cover of darkness, they would have destroyed the enemy's air force on the ground—I would then have called upon 500,000 of Chiang Kai-chek's troops, sweetened by two U.S. Marine divisions. These would have formed into two amphibious forces."

Landing north of the Red Chinese, the amphibians would have squeezed the enemy between themselves and the U.S. 8th army. "The enemy," so MacArthur told Considine, "would have been starved out within 10 days." Would Russia have intervened? "Not," said MacArthur, "over an endless one-track railroad."

—*Christian Beacon*, June 5, 1969

The Simplex Complex is what makes the representatives of the right like William Buckley seem essentially beside the point, no matter how astute their analyses. On the left the situation is exactly the reverse. Left-wing Simplex souls always seem immediately relevant, no matter how peripheral their arguments.

The reason is that Simplex Complex sufferers on the left don't really believe there has *been* a past. They may pretend to believe there was—after all, they can't deny their birth certificates or the moldy old books in rented summer houses—but to them the past is, well . . . like going to prison. Being free of the past relieves you of an enormous burden. You're free. You have only to put away the annoying little tethers of complexity to take off and soar, up there where the air is pure.

> THOUSAND DAYS PEACE PLAN: Beginning Christmas, 1969, every nation will sign a "no war" agreement with every other nation on Earth, stating that it will not for a period of the next consecutive one thousand days, engage men in any manner of warfare. YOU can help spread word of this plan and help promote WORLD PEACE— bring about a state of NO WAR ON EARTH. Free information. . . .
>
> —Advertisement

At heart, the Simplifier on the right believes that experimentation will not work because of basic human nature. His counterpart on the left says the very opposite: experiments if undertaken will always work (if not ruined by conservatives) because the flaws in human nature are totally environmental. Both views are deeply oversimplified. But they are widely held, and they make their owners perfect patsies for the con men of ideology, of whom there is no shortage.

Slopstyle

Slopstyle, admittedly, is a marginal category. After all, the Fake, or B.S., Factor *is* sloppy by definition. Still, carelessness and imprecision figure, if only as part of the laxity, haste, and confusion that enter the communications "process."

Given the worship of factual evidence, it may seem surprising that people pay so little heed to grammar, spelling, and the meaning of words. It is less surprising when you consider that the rules governing usage stand as sentinels for the larger thing to be assaulted: meaning, for words are the sentinels of meaning. Drug the sentinels and it is easier to go about the business of making claims and statements without worrying too much about how much sense they make. The imprecision that results encourages posturing and propaganda. Take a statement from President Nixon's "United States Foreign Policy for the 1970's":

> In the first postwar decades [How many have there been?] American energies were absorbed in coping with a cycle [Why cycle?] of recurrent crises, whose fundamental origins lay in the destruction of World War II [Was World War II destroyed?] and the tensions attending the emergence of scores of new nations. [But this is to

rewrite our own version of history. "International Communism," born in the Soviet Union long before World War II, was supposed to be the cause of the trouble.] Our opportunity—and challenge— is to get at the causes of crises [Surely the President can do better than "getting at" in so serious a context], to take a longer view [of carefulness, among other things], and to help build the international relationships that will provide the framework [*framework*?] of durable peace.

If you feel bad about yourself you might take to drink or pills, with the result that you might feel worse about yourself than ever. The same thing is happening in language. It gets sloppier and uglier because our brains are sloppier and less precise. And the imprecision in words makes it easier to have sloppy thoughts, as George Orwell pointed out.

Sophistry

To act craftily, to deceive purposely in debate, is the meaning of Sophistry that has come down to us. It is true that this conception is rather hard on the ancient Sophists, who, after all, perfected the dialectical argument. It is not too hard when applied to the baby Sophists who inhabit the ad agencies and public relations outfits. Here is Sophistry in advertising to end all Sophistry in advertising—which it won't:

> Come.
> We will [*sic*] be your wings. We will [*sic*] set you free.
> Free beyond the heights of man. Free to chase the sun.
> Hug a cloud.
> And, though you were born on earth [*sic*].
> To live on earth. You will be at home,
> here [*sic*] in the sky.
> The comfort and ease [???] you own [*sic*] on earth,
> you will [*sic*] have up here [*sic*].
> And Eastern will make it so.
> It shall be a most natural thing. For you.
> To fly.
> EASTERN   The Wings of Man

This exercise in Daedalusmanship probably won a prize and its author is proud to have it in his "display book." Indeed, it must have taken a genius of sorts to cram so much verbal offal, so much error in sense and grammar, into so small a package, as if all the techniques of nonsense-micronics had been successfully applied. At least, though, Eastern does not carry hydrogen bombs.

Another big producer of Sophistry is the United States military. The Air Force calls itself the "Wings of Man" too. The United States Army Intelligence School, charged with giving courses in torture, manages to call itself USAINTS. The very habit of naming weapons systems after ancient gods—Thor, Poseidon, Neptune—involves more than a touch of Sophistry. After all, gods were civilizing constructs, and to identify nuclear weapon systems with them is deeply, perhaps disgustingly, Sophistical.

Sophistry emerges in the many arguments that seem objective but in fact are cunningly one-sided. Speaking for the National Association of Broadcasters, its chairman, William Walbridge, commenting on the notion that the air waves belong to the public, is thoroughly Sophistical when he says: "There is no phrase so apt for the glib detractor, so useful for the demagogue, so sly for the covetous competitor, so relevant for the cynical revolutionary." *Christian Economics*, like many other exponents of its viewpoint, uses "freedom" Sophistry in arguing that "freedom" to keep people out of neighborhoods "is the best possible answer. It will encounter less resistance and please more people, black and white." George Meany, President of the AFL-CIO, argues that the number of skilled nonwhites in the building trades is insufficient to permit massive hiring. Why are there so few qualified nonwhites? Because the unions refused, and continue to refuse, to train them. Analysis: Sophistry.

The best defense against Sophistry is to be aware of the self-interested quality of many statements. But there are those in no position to defend themselves because they are helpless. A good example comes from the New York City Board of Education. Insisting publicly that scholarship must be given its due, it issued the following private directive to teachers:

> c. Honor Marks—
>   1. Marks for students in Honor (H) classes should be 85% or higher.
>   2. Marks for students in High Honor classes (XH) should generally not be lower than 90%.
> d. "G" (general) Marks—no mark may be given above 80% for students in "G" classes. The symbol "G" is to be added to marks of pupils in such classes officially designated as "G" classes.

In other words, once a student was in a given class he stayed there, and could not be graded higher than the specifications for his class allowed. And without higher grades, it is obviously hard to move up.

Or busing. According to former HEW official Leon E. Panetta, who quit over the busing issue:

> How can one word—busing—I will say it again—busing—frighten into craven retreat so many leaders who know that the issue is not busing. It is desegregation itself that is at issue, and busing is the symbol foisted on the Nation by those who moved into the leadership vacuum. . . . Less than 3% of the desegregation plans our office has accepted called for additional busing. Most of the districts we have dealt with to date have bused black children for miles—as many as 75 miles a

day—to take them past white schools to an inferior education! . . . Busing is a phony issue, and when you buy it as *the* issue, you are buying a shabby bill of goods.

Another HEW dropout, Paul M. Rilling, added, "Total busing mileage, in fact, decreases in most Southern States as desegregation takes place."

No critics of these nominees [Carswell, Haynsworth, Fortas] have ever come up with anything solid that was out of line with what one might naturally expect to find in the background of any active American in his fifties. Naturally a smart, successful, politically minded lawyer like Abe Fortas is going to do a bit of wheeling and dealing and talk things over with his political friends even if they happen to be Presidents. Naturally nearly all active Americans have picked up a few shares of stock as they've gone along, bought or sold some real estate, joined the local clubs, drawn up contracts (if they're lawyers) embodying the intentions of their clients and communities. Nothing fraudulent or venal or immoral has been uncovered. Rated for probity and competence, none of these three would sit at the bottom of the present court.

—*National Review Bulletin*

If this is true, should the court be called *Supreme*?

A New York City judge, Harold Rothwax (formerly a professor of law), remembers an incident in the courtroom when he was a defense lawyer. Rothwax was irked because there was always a pitcher of water on the prosecution's table but never one on the table of the defense. Unjust! Rothwax decided one day, and he requested that a pitcher of water be placed in front of the defense as well. Motion denied. Well, Rothwax asked, might he bring his own pitcher of water? Motion denied. Why? he inquired. "Because," the judge told him, "the defendant might be tempted to throw water at the judge." Has this ever happened? Rothwax asked. Has water ever been hurled at the judicial presence? "No," said the judge, "because there's never been a pitcher of water to throw."

Thermopolitical Rhetoric

In Thermopolitics, light is converted to heat. The Thermopolitical crucible softens the old, hard-edged forms so that they can be twisted into new, sometimes grotesque shapes. Thermopolitics tends toward what physicists call "the heat death," the melting down of everything into the same liqueous mass.

In the Thermopolitical process, light, in the form of an idea, is fed into a special prism, called a spokesman, which bends and distorts the light so that what emerges bears no resemblance to that which originally entered. The product is hotter, flatter, mushier, massier, messier. For example, the idea "encouraging children to be self-reliant and independent," with an honorable history and at least some empirical validity, was directed at a prism, Vice President Agnew, from whom the Thermopolitical version emerged. The country, he said, was too *permissive* with its young.

By no means confined to politicians, Thermopolitics describes a broad social phenomenon. Thermopolitics can be reduced to three fundamental laws, bearing on rhetoric.

First Law: Cant Produces Countercant

Noise is intense in the public forum as groups engage in competition with other groups for money, fame, votes, legislation, and other rewards. The endless appetite of the media for news puts a premium on novelty, excitement, and conflict. "Media solutions," which often bear no resemblance to solutions that would work in the real world, are offered by spokesmen, for which reporters provide a conduit.

Thus, cant is often relied upon as a substitute for organization, strength, a policy, or even a clear point of view. Consider how words are used by the liberal Democrats. The traditional machinery of the Democratic Party has broken down; yet liberals are frequently estranged from what is left of it. Having no organizational strength of their own, they use rhetoric to simulate solidarity. Observe that when a liberal Democratic spokesman uses words like "peace," "Vietnam," "black people," or "Nixon," he is not required to spell out positions (and frequently avoids doing so). The words are name badges reading LIBERAL DEMOCRAT. Unity on the positions is secondary because it is assumed. When the time comes for spelling out the positions, it is discovered that there has been no agreement and unity is lacking. The quantity of rhetoric has been directly proportional to the lack of action.

Many groups resort to cant as a substitute for their real deficiencies. As a result, inflated verbal coinage passes into general circulation, especially since one group cannot afford to be outspent by another, and the chances of serious "dialogue" become increasingly remote. Dialogue may not be of much use to begin with, but at least it offers hope of ideas exchanged, compromises arrived at, just claims honored. Rival monologues bellowed simultaneously eliminate these possibilities.

Second Law: Social groups are generally in disarray. To protect themselves from other groups,

*especially the groups just below them, groups will
attempt to convey an appearance of interior order
and purpose they do not possess.*

Things look worse from the inside, and not merely
because insiders exaggerate the importance of back-
stairs secrets or fail to see the over-all significance;
often, or usually, things *are* worse inside, objectively.

Groups have rivals in other groups which want to
supplant them, change their ways, take some or all of
their prerogatives, or assume their functions. If the
first group is doing as good a job as can be expected, or
is entitled in some other way to its privileges, the claims
of the challengers naturally carry less weight. The first
group tries to look as good as it can to neutralize or
refute the claims of the second.

For this reason, the collective rhetoric always por-
trays the group's purposeful activity and inner order.
To the group immediately below it, a group tries to show
an underside as dazzling (and opaque) as a mirror in
sunlight. Established bureaucratic ways are presented
as the best and only ways. Organized labor says that
nobody could do better for the workingman, or for the
unskilled, unorganized, unwhite. Less radical groups
tell more radical groups that the more radical line is
politically unrealistic. Women who express dissatis-
faction with conventional female roles are confronted
with the smooth, contented face of the family or the
notion that the male caste is stronger. The contrast
between what is presented as the disorder and anarchy
of the black slums and the tree-lined peace of the white
suburbs works against the claims of the blacks.

Within the established groups there may indeed be
great disorder, savage infighting, confusion about objectives, loss of nerve, and failure of purpose—indeed,

the same weaknesses and difficulties the established groups accuse the others of and use as a justification for staying on top. The problems of the establishment are never admitted because to do so would undermine the establishment group's claim to superiority.

The energy used to maintain appearances, conceal flaws, and deflate the claims of others heats up the rhetoric. The alternative, opening up and letting in the others, is unacceptable because it would mean change.

> *Third Law: Social institutions will change only at the speed required to protect them from attack— slowly or fast to the degree required, but usually slowly. They will put off change as long as possible. Even pretending to change is preferable to change. Left to their own devices they would never change at all. Change, in any case, is hard, and difficulty makes people impatient.*

Change, in other words, is the last thing institutions want, no matter how much they say they want it. The number of reasons why change is unattractive is almost infinite, but two deserve special mention. The first is that many groups seek a monopoly on what they do as a strictly economic matter. This is rarely, if ever, admitted. In other words, established salaries and positions are an issue even in groups that claim to want change the most. The second is the difficulty of thinking things out in the first place and the reluctance to undergo the torture again. Once an institution has decided on an approach and a philosophy, it will not alter unless forced by other people or by circumstances. Even then, it won't change as much as it says it is changing.

The Third Law is vital to an understanding of Thermopolitics because, though change is said to be both constant and necessary, the natural inertia and

stubbornness of institutions make rapid change unlikely. Faced with challenges, the institution will point
to its flexibility. It will redecorate its headquarters or
redesign its emblem. It will present fancy plans for the
renovation of the inner city or complicated legislation
for reform, and yet one looks a decade later to see what
has actually happened—not much.

Our First Law suggests that rising rhetoric replaces
action; the Second, that rhetoric is often really directed
against rivals, instead of toward achieving objective
goals; and the Third, that change is hard in the first
place. The sequence results in a kind of vicious spiral:
the failure to change (meaning to progress) produces
frustration, a further rise in the rhetoric, further
rhetorical defensiveness, and further promises of
change.

Undistributed Outlook

To the Greek logicians, a common and grievous fallacy was the undistributed middle—referring not to a paunch but to the use of a term as though it included all the members of a group when it does not. Examples of the undistributed middle can be heard nightly at the neighborhood saloon: All Communists are bad/ All Russians are Communists/ All Russians are bad. This is a very simple kind of fallacy. An army of Polish jokes rests on it. The Undistributed Outlook is more subtle.

An outlook becomes undistributed when key terms in the argument are applied unequally to different entities. Moscow's telephone troubles are due to public ownership; New York's, to unskilled labor, rapid expansion of demand, etc.—never to private ownership, just as Moscow's are never due to unskilled labor, rapid expansion of demand, etc. Chile confiscates private property, but here private property is condemned under "eminent domain" (and often paid for at well below the market rates).

The hold the Undistributed Outlook has upon Americans was apparent during President Nixon's trip to China. Visiting a glassware factory, Mrs. Nixon asked, "Do they [the workers] use their own judgment on what they mix together? Can they just take a little bit of this and a little bit of that?"

> Mrs. Chao Mei-yun, the roly-poly chairman of the factory's revolutionary committee, took care of that bit of bourgeois fantasy with a simple, firm reply: "They have a certain design."*

As if American factory workers could take a little of this and a little of that, and didn't have a "certain design" to follow.

Words alone are often enough to indicate that the Undistributed Outlook lurks in the background. Take a comparison of the phrases used by the newspapers to describe men and women:

writer	lady writer
professor	woman professor
worried businessman	harried housewife
old man	little old lady
henpecked	dominated
complain	nag
protest	complain
angry	hysterical/strident
courageous man	tough little woman
man	wife/mother/grandmother/ girl†

On the other hand, women's outlook can be undistributed too. "We have women's prisons but we don't have a women's museum. Why not?" said a woman artist.

Observe that words like "typical" or "average" often indicate the Undistributed Outlook, because they mean

---

* *The New York Times*, February 24, 1972, p. 1.
† Sheila Tobias, "Newspaper Guidelines," paper (n.d.), p. 4.

typical or average in respect to something particular. According to *A Guide to Charitable Giving:*

> To help explain the life income contract let's take a typical example. Suppose Mr. and Mrs. Jones are a couple who have retired. Living on investments totalling $1,000,000, they receive an average annual income of $35,000. After income taxes of $10,000, their net income is $25,000 a year.

Because of the Undistributed Outlook, a person sees reality only in his own terms and accuses others of doing exactly what he is doing. Take Robert Welch, founder of the John Birch Society. In castigating the radicals for obscenity, he referred to "Mother Fokker's Soul Food Specialties." "A tough, dedicated Communist," says the anti-Communist as he takes up arms. Often, the Undistributed Outlook can be made apparent by reversal of the terms. "Obviously, the Communist leaders believed they were winning in the South. With things presumably going their way, they had no interest in a peaceful settlement, or compromise of any description. They slammed the door on our peace offer," wrote President Johnson. *But,* reverse this: Obviously, the American leaders believed they were winning in the South. With things presumably going their way, they had not the slightest interest in a peaceful settlement, or compromise of any description.

Doubt-Benefiting figures heavily in the Undistributed Outlook, because, usually, you give Doubt-Benefits to your side. The same issue of *The New York Times Magazine* contained both an article called "Attorney General John Mitchell: 'The Justice Department Is an Institution for Law Enforcement, Not Social Change'" and another titled "Brezhnev Sets the Clock Back."

Both officials, it turned out, were engaged in retrogressions of a strikingly similar order. The *Times*, it seems, gave Mitchell the benefit of the doubt.

Doubt-Benefits are almost always employed against wage increases. The same executive who finds a forty-five-dollar-a-month raise for employees "scandalously high" or "precipitate" would find the same raise for himself scandalous too—scandalously low.

Doubt-Benefits were always awarded to the American free-enterprise system when it was said that no other system could provide so well for its citizens. This view, though, left out of account a number of factors having to do with resources, geography, freedom from war, etc., and the fact that in our era other systems had to start from much further back. An insight into the Undistributed Outlook as held by Americans is provided by continued reiterations that Americans consume the lion's share of the world's resources.

> With only one-fifteenth of the world's population and about the same proportion of the world's area and natural resources, the United States has more than half the world's telephone, telegraph and radio networks—more than three-quarters of the world's automobiles—almost half the world's radios —and consumes more than half the world's copper and rubber, two-thirds of the silk, a quarter of the coal and nearly two-thirds of the crude oil.
> —Business advertisement, 1950's

The self-centeredness of this attitude is easily revealed by its neglect of the corollary—that if Americans use such a high percentage of global resources, the rest of the world is not using them. That the rest of the world is not using resources which in good measure come from elsewhere than the United States may, in the long run, prove to be a more important fact than that America *is* using them. But, as Americans looked at things, we were the standard by which measurements were taken.

Or, take the Kennedy Administration's concept of "counterinsurgency." "Insurgency" assumes someone is an "insurgent," and you will "counter" him. If "counterinsurgency" failed in Vietnam, one reason was that the "insurgents" did not share the view that they were insurgents. They were not to be lightly persuaded that they resembled, in the dictionary description, "a treasonous rabble below the level of a revolution." Because they didn't regard themselves in this way, they did not *act* as insurgents were thought to, much to the embarrassment of American policymakers. Sooner or later the ludicrous pictures of the world that spring from the Undistributed Outlook become apparent—but after the fighting is over.

A million empty cigarette packs were collected in 1972 by compassionate citizens to pay for open-heart surgery for a two-year-old girl from Crown Point, New York, in the mistaken belief that tobacco companies redeem the packs at a penny each. How sad! We tolerate the lack of medical protection for the society (and our representatives vote against it), and yet we will go to almost any length to help an individual, especially a child. Only an Undistributed Outlook could fail to grasp the irony.

Upbeat Endings

> SIDNEY: Yes . . . weep now, darling, weep. Let us both weep. That is the first thing: to let ourselves feel again. . . . Then, tomorrow, we shall make something strong of this sorrow. . . . (*They sit spent, almost physically drained and motionless . . . as the clear light of morning gradually fills the room.*) Curtain.
> —LORRAINE HANSBERRY, *The Sign in Sidney Brustein's Window*

Ah yes, the happy ending. No matter that a million people starve in Bangladesh; the sun has started to shine again. America may be at the crossroads, but we will, you can be sure, with intelligence and determination, choose the right road. "The remedy is the same as in 1776 or 1787—to rediscover our overarching values, to recommit ourselves to them, to restructure our institutions to fulfill them, and to support and sustain leaders who will serve them. Who will emerge as the Franklin, Washington, Jefferson, Adams or Madison of our time?"* Could it be, no one?

Upbeat endings, you suspect, are composed after the rest of the book is written. "Got to give them something

---

* James MacGregor Burns, *Uncommon Sense*. New York: Harper & Row, 1972, p. 181.

to cheer them on," you can almost hear the author say. The trouble with Upbeat Endings is that, in urging us onward and upward, they attempt to make us forget what was making us unhappy in the first place.

This was discovered by Charles D. Hepler, publisher of *Reader's Digest*, a periodical whose zealous optimism is closer in spirit to that of the liberal intellectuals than many of the latter care to admit. Hepler was addressing businessmen. He told them that the ultimate enemy of society is "pessimism . . . the virus that infects our subconscious and that, I believe, could pin the will of business leaders against the wall. . . . Let us infuse our conversation, our letters, our memos and phone calls with optimism. Let's talk about the future in terms of its promise—not its pitfalls." Perhaps the reminder is cruel, but shortly thereafter Hepler was stabbed by his son.

Verbicide

Verba volant, says the Latin: words fly away. Today they do not have the chance to fly—instead, they are murdered.

No one seems to know just why language changes as it does.* An educated guess is that changes in language are deeply related to social change and social events. The cheapening of verbal coin through linguistic inflation may be tied to monetary inflation. The verbicide in Vietnam may have been connected to the herbicide practiced there. In 1970, a U.S. "task force" observed that it was "an almost hopeless task" to learn what the South Vietnamese thought of the American "presence" because of the language barrier. The American explanations of the war suggested that Americans had barriers to understanding it *in their own language*.

---

* "The unceasing processes of change in language are mainly unconscious. The results of change may rise to the recognition of the speakers; the acts of change, and especially its causes, happen without awareness of those through whose minds and mouths they take place. This holds true of all departments of the language; the phonetics, the structural form, largely even the meaning of the words. When a change has begun to creep in, it may be resisted on the ground of being incorrect or vulgar or foreign. But the underlying motives of the objectors are apparently as unknown to themselves as are the impulses of the innovators."—A. L. Kroeber, *Anthropology*. New York: Harcourt, Brace, 1936, p. 125.

Freighted with cant words, pseudo words and non-words, the American tongue has taken off, and take-offs do not always "eventuate" in successful landings. Closely analyzed, the trends affecting the language seem to be these: incessant repetition (due to word fads), uglification, and devolution.

Repetition: Try saying a word over and over again and see how the meaning drains out of it, as though an artery had been cut. Many words might have led long and useful lives except for the writers of advertising, book-jacket copy, public relations pieces, political speeches, and so on, who have abused them mercilessly, with no restraint shown and no quarter given. Words ought to be protected from human predators like some rare species of wildlife. They are not, and "affluent," "achieving," "distinguished," "important," "unquestionable," "celebrate," "career," "identity," "great," "belonging," "enjoy," "awareness," ad infinitum, have been killed off like buffalo.

"Creative" is another word that has been badly abused (a California university offers a course in "Remedial Creativity"). Why did "creativity" become a cliché? Not, certainly, because it stood for innovation. The very repetition of this word to the exclusion of others that might have conveyed a closer meaning is the absence of creativity. "Creative" as a cant word indicates conformity. What is happening to the language may well approximate what may be happening to the *users* of the language—increasingly narrowed, routinized, mass-produced.

Uglification: Not all words can be expected to shimmer like sunbeams, but when there's a choice between Anglo-Saxon sprightliness and latinized leadenness, between words that bounce and those hyphenated or

dumbbell versions of them, the latter are often chosen:
"work-fare," "peace dividend," "wilderness systems,"
"productive member of society," "defoliate." The uglification of language expresses, perhaps, not only a
sense that the environment is ugly or that the action is
ugly but an approach that is heavy-handed and often
pretentious. Language is used like a chore you would
be happy to be rid of; there is little joy in it. The problems in the language may show that, for all the "problem-solving," problems are not being solved.

Devolution (or retrograde evolution): The instincts
of the young may be much admired, but the trouble is
that a vast number of young people, as both studies
and observation show, can't *write* or *speak* with anything like proficiency. Though some believe it to be a
form of stuttering, the frequent use of "er . . ." or
"like . . ." may also be a way to show that the user so
distrusts the vocabulary that he is shopping around to
see if precise words are still in manufacture. Or is the
er-er or like-er buying time to see if any words occur to
him at all? This is a fairly literate version of the new
speech:

> I mean, we all know this but the kids still look at it
> like it's something weird or holy or something or
> don't pay any attention to it and just keep on doing
> their thing ["thing" pretense. What thing?]. This
> ponk in EVO [*East Village Other*] talked about
> Woodstock being like a hip concentration camp, or
> said something about he could dig it if there was a
> groovy camp like that where they could all do their
> own thing and not have to bother with the awful
> nasty stuff in the world.
>
> —*Rat*

The new language seems to have come into being as
protest against the sluggishness of the vocabulary in

general, and also as a means of self-identification among cult groups like the drug addicts. The rapid expropriation of the cult-words—"man," "head," "groovy," "freak-out," "turn on," "trip," "rap," "flip"— probably shows that the larger language was badly in need of pep (even though the real meaning of the new words was often not understood. Do the suburban ladies who use the phrases to show where they're *at* know that "funky" at first meant sex smells, or that "up tight" referred to the contraction of the testicles in times of stress?). The trouble with the specialized language is that it tends to devolve into a vocabulary of very few words, until a couple of words are used to convey all experience, like *fuck* and *suck*.

"Americans," said Walt Whitman,

> are going to be the most fluent and melodious-voiced people in the world—and the most perfect users of words. The new world, the new times, the new people, the new vistas need a new tongue according—yes, what is more, they will have such a new tongue—will not be satisfied until it is evolved.

Has it, in fact, evolved?

III.

the dangers of dogmatism, or, the belief explosion

THE MANY problems and fakeries discussed so far can be examined as just one: credulity. For the credulity attached to the pseudo facts, pseudo propositions, and pseudo language comprising the B.S. Factor is an important part of its acceptance by everyone.

Now, credulity does not stand alone. In turn, it is part of an attitude called dogmatism—the belief in and defense of "truth." Those who believe strongly in "truth" will try to find it through the mechanism of belief. We see today a "belief explosion" which throws skepticism to the winds and attaches itself in a credulous manner to mental malpractice and intellectual humbuggery of every kind—to faking it, small and big. Without dogmatism, the Fake Factor could not exist. Because of dogmatism, that ancient enemy, anything goes, or very nearly.

Two kinds of dogmatists can be dismissed from consideration at the beginning. One is the artful or dramatic dogmatist, who uses dogmatism only for effect —for laughs or to drive home a point. A dogmatist of this kidney is Robert Townsend, author of *Up the Organization* ("Don't hire Harvard Business School graduates," he says cheerfully). The other kind of dogmatist who may not really mean it is the official, or ceremonial, dogmatist. For some reason, dogmatism is not only sanctioned but absolutely demanded in proclamations of Mother's Day or dedications of a new bridge.

The kind of dogmatist who must be looked at with alarm is the one who firmly believes that he owns a corner of the truth. Roughly, real dogmatists come in three kinds: overt, intermediate, and covert (including dogmatists of theory). An overt dogmatist can be easily recognized. Jabbing his finger, he is likely to say, "The truth is," "Without question," "Obviously," "Totally," "Conclusively," "Rest assured," "No one can dispute." This sort of dogmatist is a familiar figure at the local bar, behind the wheel of a taxicab, and in high places. President Nixon has used most of these phrases in his press conferences.

Although an overt dogmatist seldom changes, the subjects that he is dogmatic about do. You rarely hear, for instance, the dogmas of capitalism like this one from 1948:

> If every Communist knew what every sane person in a capitalist country knows—the high standard of living which capitalism makes possible, the pride of individual accomplishment, the satisfaction of knowing you can go as far as your own abilities and ambitions will take you, the security of justice, the joy of knowing your son can go even farther than you have gone . . . if every Com-

munist knew the facts about capitalism, there wouldn't be any Communists.

—Advertisement

But there are newer dogmas:

It is the *function* of men to oppress. It is the *function* of men to exploit. It is the *function* of men to *lie,* and to *betray,* and to *humiliate,* to *crush,* to *ignore,* and the final *insult:* it is the *function* of men to tell women that *man's iniquities* are *woman's function!*

—TI-GRACE ATKINSON

The dangers of such flat-footed assertions are obvious. The fact that dogmatists very often turn out to be wrong does not mean they stop being dogmatists. What many of them have done, however, is develop a style that is meant to conceal the dogmatism. They use words like "incline toward," "in my opinion," "maybe," "perhaps," "I think," without for a moment abandoning their truth-corner. Dogmatists of this, the intermediate, kind account for the eerie quality of many cocktail-party conversations with two confirmed dogmatists busily protesting "Don't you think that," "Couldn't it be," "But I wonder if" without changing, or exchanging, a single idea.

An intelligent dogmatist, however, would no more reveal his persuasion than a devil-worshiper in the Middle Ages. He won't be burned at the stake, but he knows that dogmatism is neither a convincing style of argument nor good manners, and he shuns phrases like "in my opinion" because the cover they offer is too thin. The smart dogmatist has mastered the dogmatic dodges to the point where his dogmatism is so well hidden that only close inspection will unmask it. You can, it seems, teach an old dogmatist new tricks.

Let us note some ways to recognize the disguised dogmatist. One is to look for dogmatic words that have been skillfully bootlegged. Take a statement by Maurice Stans. "The greatness of our free enterprise system rests on the fact that its potential is virtually unlimited. That's the cornerstone of our democracy." The uncritical individual might find this statement unexceptionable, but wait. Stans has slyly introduced the word "fact." A potential is not a fact, because if it were a fact it would not be a potential. That this "potential" is virtually unlimited is an opinion, rest assured. That democracy rests on free enterprise is a judgment, nothing more. Note here another dogmatic device, the use of words like "cornerstone" (or "keystone," "foundation," "watershed," "building block") which are meant to convince that the truth conveyed is as solid and factual as a physical thing.

Another clue to the disguised dogmatist is his method of arguing from a single cause. (Democracy is the result of free enterprise.) Single-cause arguments are automatically suspect because in real life little or nothing happens as a result of only one thing. Dogmatists like single causes, though, because they make for the pat answers and formulas the dogmatist feels comfortable with. An example is the rotten-apple theory of police corruption: a few bad cops cause the trouble; get rid of the bad cops and you've "eliminated the source of corruption." What accounts for the bad cops? It must be human nature and/or general conditions, in which case the bad cops you fire will be replaced by other bad cops.

Dogmatists deal in half-, quarter-, and so on down to zero-truths with the same assurance. In fact, the assurance with which a statement is delivered is another clue to the dogmatic personality. Take a statement by Vice President Agnew (a dogmatist par excellence) about "the liberal community, who are [sic] presently [sic] so blinded by total dedication to individual freedom that they [sic] cannot see the steady erosion of collective freedom." This sounds as though it might at least be a debatable point until you inquire what "collective freedom" is. Can freedom be "collective"? Not likely. By "collective freedom" Agnew has hidden his true meaning, "majority will." That the "liberal community" cannot recognize what the majority wants is a questionable statement all around. It is also a rather scary one, since it implies that individual freedom is counter to what the majority wishes.

When we were young, dogmatists were easier to recognize because we dealt with simpler material then and everybody knew which kid on the block was a know-it-all. Then the know-it-all went to graduate or law school or into politics and matured into a dogmatist of theory. He became Scammon and Wattenberg:

> . . . the clear emergence of a new and major Voting Issue in America, an issue so powerful that it may rival bimetallism and depression in American voting history, an issue powerful enough that under certain circumstances it can compete in political potency with the older economic issues. We call this force the Social Issue. . . .*

---

* Richard M. Scammon and Ben J. Wattenberg, *The Real Majority*. New York: Coward-McCann, 1970, p. 49.

Or Alvin Toffler:

> To understand what is happening to us as we move
> into the age of super-industrialism, we must
> analyze the process of acceleration and confront
> the concept of transcience. If acceleration is a new
> social force, transcience is its psychological coun-
> terpart, and without an understanding of the role
> it plays in contemporary human behavior, all our
> rhetorics of personality, all our psychology, must
> remain pre-modern. Psychology without the con-
> cept of transcience cannot take account of precisely
> those phenomena that are peculiarly contempo-
> rary.*

Or Norman Mailer, in *The New York Times Magazine:*

> The face of the solution may reside in the notion
> that the Left has been absolutely right on some
> critical problems of our time, and the Conservatives
> have been altogether correct about one enormous
> matter—which is that the Federal Government has
> absolutely no business whatever in local affairs.

Dogmatists of theory are the hardest of all to detect
because they seem to be only airing their views. But
there is a difference between ideas that are offered, with
some caution, for the purpose of being scrutinized and
argued with and those which are simply *served*, like a
TV dinner. The dogmatist dishes out his theory without
reservation. He requires of you an act of belief.

Now, the dogmatist, of any sort, is one who does not
readily accept the highly conditional and contingent
nature of reality. He deals in *truth*. This forces him to
divide things up into what is certainly true and what
certainly isn't. Because of his truth-belief, he works

---

* *Future Shock*. New York: Random House, p. 19.

from fixed systems and doctrines from which he inter-
prets things. He tries to eliminate uncertainty in any
way he can. He is likely to be slow to change and not
experimental, unlike his opposite number, the skeptic.

The prevalence of dogmatism has led to the belief explosion in which everybody *believes* something (or feels
like a pinhead if he doesn't). The accent on true belief
as a necessary function of life has encouraged the
creation of ideas to believe *in,* ideas that are held to be
true on dogmatic grounds alone. By professors as well
as preachers, researchers as well as radicals, ideas are
expounded as though they were revealed truth and not
the more humble stuff of opinion.

The fall-out from the belief explosion often consists
of dubious assertions, quickly promulgated and eagerly
grabbed. No one can live very long without becoming
aware that dubious assertions are almost mass-produced; you could fill a Sears catalogue with such as
these: "The students who burned the Bank of America
in Santa Barbara may have done more towards saving
the environment than all the Teach-ins put together"
(*Ramparts*). ". . . ideologically directed positions are
basically irrelevant where experts are available" (As in
the Soviet Union?) (Daniel Bell). "It is quite as immoral to kill ten human beings as a hundred thousand"
(Governor Nelson Rockefeller—paraphrase). "Think
in terms of total control of the U.S." ("Black Mani-
festo"). "Communists labor ceaselessly to exploit the
racial strife and violence in this country. . . . One
main communist goal is to alienate Negroes from established authority" (J. Edgar Hoover). "In one way or
another, all the major problems facing you derive from
the erosion of the authority of the institutions of American society" (Daniel Patrick Moynihan). "Either ecology

action is revolutionary action or it is no action at all"
(a good prescription for inaction). . . .

As a practical matter, when you start packaging
truths you are aiding and abetting the practice of
fakery. Instead of admitting you have guesses, attitudes, points of view, you start selling beliefs in the
market place, and the result is a climate of certitude
and credulity in which fakery flourishes. And out of
that atmosphere come precisely those dogmatic judgments about the nature of the Communist monolith,
the mentality of "middle America" or the blacks, about
"postindustrial society" and the significance of Vietnam
which have led the country into an endless series of
misconceptions and horrendous mistakes. A dogmatic
past cannot be undone, but at least we can work toward
a skeptical future.

In the meantime, if an applicant tells you he's a
"problem-solver" or a "decision-maker," don't give him
the job. He'll be solving problems that aren't problems
and making decisions that don't need making. Never
hire a dogmatist.

IV.

behind the faking, or, the nonsense explosion

αT LEAST since the early years of the nineteenth century—longer, perhaps, if one is to put a strict interpretation on things—American expression has been marked by a streak of rhetorical flamboyancy and even excessiveness. This streak of rogue rhetoric may be narrow, but it runs deep. Foreign observers were keenly aware of it—more so than Americans. Tocqueville referred to our "pompous and inflated style." Fifty years later, Lord Bryce went further:

> Public taste, which was high in the days before the Revolution, when it was formed and controlled by a small number of educated men, began to degenerate in the first half of this century. Despite the influence of several orators of the first rank, incessant stump speaking and the inordinate vanity of the average audience brought a florid and inflated style into fashion. . . .*

_____

* *The American Commonwealth* (1888), Vol. II, p. 801.

There are those (a minority, to be sure) who believe that the superficiality attending much American rhetoric was and remains a reflection of certain properties of mind linked in turn to our political institutions. H. Mark Roelofs, a political scientist, describes the Constitution's "compulsive pluralism, based on a Hobbesian theory of natural antagonism between men."

> The result has been a kind of built-in mindlessness whose purpose is to trade off one interest against another, with serious cooperation for social ends all but ruled out. The American system was never designed to work the way it claims to work. Its very superficiality was meant as a safeguard. Stability was the object and nonsense the inevitable consequence.*

By the age of Jackson and the Common Man, at least, the roots of the rogue rhetoric were established in the "tall talk" of the frontier. "The egalitarianism and populism and anti-intellectualism of American politics takes over then," says the historian John William Ward.

> It was not a matter of the extension of the suffrage. Rather, it was the destruction of elite politics based on generations of leadership by the "better sort," by the sudden expansion of the country which sent people moving (westward into the continent, but, just as important, inward toward the towns and cities and factories of the new industrial civilization). The transportation revolution and the emergence of a national market economy forced the emergence of national political parties and the need to appeal to a national electorate. The result was to shift political discourse from particular and

---

* Interview.

> concrete issues to high-flown rhetoric and spread-eagle bombast.*

Here, for instance, is how a politician, circa 1840, talked about the need for public schools and greater educational opportunity.

> When the children of toil are as much shunned in society as if they were leprous convicts just emerged from loathsome cells, the most powerful obstacle is erected between them and all that can make them estimable and happy. The family tie of the race is snapped asunder. . . .

Exaggeration, self-upmanship, or "boosterism," as Professor Daniel J. Boorstin calls it, immortalized in the humor of Mark Twain, was common on the frontier. Boorstin writes: "In so expansive an era, the old boundaries—between fact and wish, between the indicative and the optative, between the present and the future—no longer served."

> The word "tall" in England had long meant simply "high" or "lofty," and in this sense "tall talk" would have meant the opposite of "small talk." In America, the word "tall" meant not only high or lofty, but "unusual," "remarkable," or "extravagant." And these were precisely the dimensions of the American experience. . . . Tall talk described the penumbra of the familiar. It blurred the edges of fact and fiction. Discovered and established by urgent need and quick consent, tall talk was a language without inhibitions. It did not grow, it exploded from sudden popular demand for modes of speech more vague, less clear edged than the

---

* Letter to the author.

existing language provided . . . It was needed because the Old World notion of exaggeration had
itself become inadequate.*

It is not pushing history too much to suggest that the
rhetorical skills developed on the frontier would serve
the South, in arguments for slavery before the Civil War
and for white supremacy after it; would serve to justify
the forced migration of the Indians; would serve the
railroads in their land grabs; would serve those who ex-
ploited the immigrants by instilling in them boundless
gratitude; would serve the interests of those who
profited from American incursions into Cuba and the
banana republics of Latin America; would serve those
who tried to prevent the development of the trade
unions. In other words, the Fake Factor, even in its
comparatively primitive phases, was not mere rhetoric
but was fast becoming a way of making specious or
selfish arguments and actions look sound, justifiable,
and even generous. And each new adventure in rhetoric
gained experience for the next.

Conventionally, historians have interpreted the inflationary cast of the American mind as a part of the
famous American optimism, assuming American excessiveness to be part of an expansiveness tailored to
the size of the American endeavor. As Henry Steele
Commager observed, "The American had spacious ideas,
his imagination roamed a continent, and he was impatient with petty transactions, hesitations, and timidi-
ties . . . this . . . tended to give a quantitative cast
to his thinking and inclined him to place a quantitative
valuation upon almost everything."† Yet so far as

* *The Americans: The National Experience.* New York: Vintage
Books, 1965, pp. 290–91.
† *The American Mind.* New Haven: Yale, 1950, pp. 6–7.

American rhetoric depended on the use of fallacious arguments, so far as the urge to make things look big, shiny, grand, and good was based on pretense, exaggeration, and even sophistry, was it not related to the logical and rhetorical fallacies identified by Greek and subsequent philosophers? Was this streak of rogue rhetoric, this verbal (and mental) gene, more or less inherited in the manner suggested by the logician Stephen Toulmin: "It is conceivable that unsound methods of argument could retain their hold in a society, and be passed on down the generations, just as much as constitutional bodily deficiency or a defect in individual psychology"?

But for this devious strain to loom ever larger in the national psyche, communications technology had to advance to a point where what we have identified as the B.S. Factor could be applied to the people as a whole, where everybody could be on the receiving end, and this meant wireless, radio, TV, the mass distribution of books, newspapers, magazines; advertising, public relations; the computer print-out—all the means by which messages are sent. Mass communications made possible what Walter Lippmann referred to as "the insertion between man and his environment of a pseudo-environment. To that pseudo-environment his behavior is a response. . . . For certainly, at the level of social life, what is called the adjustment of man to his environment takes place through the medium of fiction.*

For Lippmann, the fictions that lay at the heart of the widespread fakery were a more or less inevitable result of reducing complex reality to symbols that could

---

* *Public Opinion*, 1922. New York: Free Press (paper), 1965, p. 10.

be understood. Going further, George Orwell accused governments of consciously using pseudo realities to justify policy, through a number of methods, among them the calculated manipulation of the vocabulary. Bertrand Russell also saw the manipulation of the masses as the problem:

> The discovery that man can be scientifically manipulated, and that governments can turn large masses this way or that as they choose, is one of the causes of our misfortunes. There is as much difference between a collection of mentally free citizens and a community moulded by modern methods of propaganda as there is between a heap of raw materials and a battleship. Education, when it was at first made universal in order that all might be able to read and write, has been found capable of serving quite other purposes. By instilling nonsense it unifies populations and generates collective enthusiasm. If all governments taught the same nonsense, the harm would not be so great. Unfortunately, each has its own brand, and the diversity serves to produce hostility between the devotees of different creeds. If there is ever to be peace in the world, governments will have to agree either to inculcate no dogmas, or all to inculcate the same.*

In American terms Orwell and Russell reckoned without an essential quality, the do-it-yourself spirit. Americans, characteristically, wouldn't have nonsense imposed from on top but would insist on conferring it upon themselves. Of course, conditions—historical, cultural—had to be right for the nonsense to reach a criti-

---

* *The Basic Writings of Bertrand Russell, 1903–1959*, edited by Robert E. Egner and Lester E. Denonn. New York: Simon and Schuster, 1961, p. 89.

cal mass, and evidently they were right after World War II, because then American rhetoric began to expand in every way. Americans suddenly engaged in an orgy of showing off, self-congratulation, and pretension, as revealed by their cars, their suburban manses, their outsized universities, and even their vocabulary, ushering in a new Gilded Age. This time, ready to help was a small army of experts in mass foolery—purveyors of sweet-sounding baby talk, concealed fallacies, misleading claims, and servile *non sequiturs*—not merely the copywriter and the publicist (in fact, they made no bones about the uses of their professions), but speech writers, compilers of annual reports, journalists, columnists, military analysts, fast-buck intellectuals, rhetorical revolutionaries, pollsters, ambitious sociologists, press secretaries, pollsters, and the like: a tribe of semantic Shylocks, novelty-mongers, kicksters, word-jugglers, theory-twirlers, who set up their electric typewriters and computers on the great American mind desert and went to work, pouring out their dubious notions, questionable dogmas, synthetic syllogisms, and captious doctrines to the delight of the inhabitants. American society not only welcomed the brazen attempt to tinker with its intelligence but wanted to participate. Thus, extensive cosmetics and even plastic surgery were applied to the body of American language and thought. Fakery took off.

As to the whys, there can be only speculation. Perhaps the "upwardly mobile" Americans secretly feared that the Great Depression would return and the rug would be pulled from under them. In other words, rhetorical excess served to ward off fear. Then, perhaps, America was playing a new role in the world. It does not seem accidental that the nonsense explosion occurred in tandem with the atomic bomb. Before World War II, American rhetoric was subdued by comparison, perhaps in keeping with a small standing army, a depression, and a foreign policy with aims so limited that it could hardly be called a foreign policy at all. This was the America, it will be remembered, that discovered delight in such sophisticated activities as marathon dancing, flagpole sitting and goldfish swallowing. . . . After the war, though, it was different. America had the bomb, an enormous army, and a felt responsibility over the globe. At this point, Americans began patting themselves and their institutions on the back in earnest. Perhaps the newly expansive rhetoric was a way of making them feel comfortable in a new role.

The Cold War brought fear as well—fear of the bomb, of the Russians, of "subversion." Fear and its cousin, cowardice, brought the late Senator Joseph R. McCarthy, perhaps the last real liar and a precursor of the B.S. Factor's most alarming uses. Himself a creature of fear, McCarthy *caused* great fear, and government officials, wishing to protect themselves, began to resort more and more to secrecy. Secrecy figures strongly in the B.S. Factor because without accurate information men are forced to guess. Guesswork is not widely respected in a culture that considers itself scientific, and so hunches and partial information were presented as hard fact. (See the newspaper versions of the Vietnam war in terms of the Pentagon Papers covering the same period.) This produced a new generation of sages and seers whose contribution to the B.S. Factor was immense. And, in any case, the Cold War, and later the Vietnam war, made deviousness and subterfuge part of official policy. The government did not want actually to lie (through fear of exposure; there remains on the part of the public a lingering attachment to truth), but it did not wish to tell the whole truth either, and that automatically put the Fake into play.

So the Fake, or B.S., Factor is interactive—it doesn't just exist by itself. This is why blaming the fakery on the quality of education tells us little, because, while popular education may have been shrewdly going about the business of lowering IQ's as the best preparation for life, students are trained to live in society, and the society, simply, needs to fake it more than ever. Let us return to the language. Language has been described as "psycho-biological"—". . . a person and his environment represent an enormous complex in which there is a tendency to maintain equilibrium; because of inevitable changes either in the individual or in his environment there must be constant readjustment in this complex to restore equilibrium; speech is one device for restoring equilibrium."* Language becomes a way of adjusting to reality. That reality might be deficient—that is, it might fail to satisfy—but even so the language would tend to adjust. There might be *dysfunctions* which the language would work to cover up, conceal, in order to avoid disequilibrium, or at least the consciousness of it. The Fake Factor would be a way of hiding our imperfections *from ourselves.*†

---

* Zipf, George Kingsley, *The Psycho-Biology of Language, An Introduction to Dynamic Philosophy.* Cambridge, Mass.: The M.I.T. Press, 1935, p. 264.
† Theoretical support for this position comes from the sociologist Leon Festinger and his "theory of cognitive dissonance." Seeking internal harmony, he theorized, the human mind attempts to reach and maintain equilibrium through reducing

The self-administered nonsense would thus serve as a kind of facade to conceal the dysfunctions of society. Fakery fragments attention in an endless maze of *non sequiturs,* blurs perception in junkthink, dulls intelligence with nonsense. It is hard to change the world when you can no longer clearly grasp its outlines—it is hard to know exactly what to be dissatisfied *about.* It follows that the *greater* the dysfunctions the *more* the B.S. Factor would come into play, because the bigger the defects of society the more the B.S. Factor would be employed to rationalize them and to uphold the *status quo.*

Among the things a society might want to conceal from itself—because the realization might be too painful, or imply a need for changes that the society did not want to, or was afraid to, make—would be the failure to achieve its own stated goals. Progress, for instance. Americans work, and work hard, but do they in any fundamental sense *progress?* And in a time-frame small enough so that progress is clearly focused? How do we measure progress? Greater personal security? Shorter work week? Better education? Improved medical protection? Higher culture? More happiness? In none of these ways does there seem to be progress com-

---

the dissonance of conflicting ideas, or cognitions. *"The presence of dissonance gives rise to pressures to reduce or eliminate the dissonance. The strength of the pressures to reduce the dissonance is a function of the magnitude of the dissonance."* (Italics his.) Dissonance increases when activities are undertaken about which one feels uncomfortable; it can be reduced by the creation of suitable rationales. In the same way, thoughts and even values can be reshaped to reduce, to tolerable levels, the dissonance caused by actions already taken (or not taken). *The Theory of Cognitive Dissonance.* Stanford, Calif.: Stanford University Press, 1957, p. 18.

mensurate with the enormous effort Americans have been putting out.*

Another kind of realization which might not want to be faced is that organized stupidity has become a necessary feature of the economy. Says the anthropologist Jules Henry, "If we were all logicians the economy would not survive and herein lies the paradox, for *in order to exist economically we must try by might and main to remain stupid.*"† According to the dollars-and-nonsense theory, Americans must be trained and regimented as idiots so that they will continue to consume products which greater clearheadedness would tell them they neither want nor need. Stupidity, in other words, means jobs.

To some, the main cause of dysfunction is the capitalist system and its inherent failures, and the strained quality of much rhetoric is the result of a refusal to face the fact.

> The morally overwrought quality of much liberal thinking derives, I believe, not merely from indignation but from the strain of trying not to perceive

---

* A good brief summary of American progress is to be found in "A Social Report in Practice," *The Public Interest,* No. 15, Spring, 1969, p. 98. It looks at progress rates under the headings of Health and Illness, Social Mobility, The Physical Environment, Housing and Poverty, Public Order and Safety, Learning, Science and Art, and Participation and Alienation. Only science seems to be advancing. For a chronicle of our "progress," see William O. Douglas, *Points of Rebellion* (New York: Random House, 1970). The remarkable (or perhaps unremarkable) aspect of Douglas' depressing findings is that the conditions he reports are so persistent. In other words, years have passed and nothing has been done about them.

† *Culture Against Man.* New York: Random House, 1963, p. 48. (Italics his.)

that capitalism's logical tendency is to preserve inequality, deplete resources, pollute the elements, keep an underclass out of work, and tyrannize over the economies of other nations. The attempt to address such problems without calling attention to property relations yields a confused, symbolic, and hortatory thinking which seizes on immediate occasions for outrage or sympathy while neglecting structural factors. Each new military intervention, if not quickly and successfully concluded, is a tragic blunder that "we" can never make again, for "we" have learned better—as if it had been our decision in the first place. Each new welfare program is an all-out war on injustice, definitive proof that "we care." Each new articulate candidate with good manners and a patrician distaste for politics will surely save our country from its real internal enemies, the uncouth rednecks and crazy generals who lack all honor and compassion.*

For the British writer Iris Murdoch, as reported in the *Times:*

Words constitute the ultimate texture and stuff of our moral being, since they are the most refined and delicate and detailed, as well as the most universally used and understood, of the symbolisms whereby we express ourselves into existence.

We become spiritual animals when we become verbal animals. The fundamental distinctions can only be made in words. Words are spirit. Of course eloquence is no guarantee of goodness, and an inarticulate man can be virtuous. But the quality of a civilization depends upon its ability to discern and reveal truth and this depends upon the scope and purity of its language.

---

* Frederick Crews, "Do Literary Studies Have an Ideology?" *Publication of the Modern Language Association*, May, 1970, p. 425.

Any dictator attempts to degrade the language because this is a way to mystify. And many of the quasi-automatic operations of capitalist industrial society tend also toward mystification and the blunting of verbal precision.

For others, the problems revealed by the rhetoric are more narrowly political: that is, the failure of the political system has produced a dysfunction in democracy. For James MacGregor Burns, the central problem of our day "is the disjunction between means and ends. It is the conduct of one line of activity on the basis of what specifically and narrowly works, and another line of rhetoric that may be designed to meet the people's need for official piety."*

We have failed because we have tried to deal with deeply entrenched, interlocked sets of national problems through sporadic, piecemeal action. We have acted in this fashion because our political institutions are disorganized and fragmented, our leaders improvising and opportunistic, our thinking pragmatic and "practical."†

We have already observed that fakery may be a means of hiding imperfections, even of trying to make society work (however clumsily) in the teeth of those imperfections, by simply ignoring the fact that they are there, or obscuring the fact in a cloud of adaptive rhetoric. If true, this means that fakery would be in the greatest demand precisely when the imperfections, or the sense of them, were greatest, or when the dysfunctions were at their strongest. The extensive use of the Fake Factor today shows that there are imperfec-

---

* Op. cit., p. 10.
† *Ibid.*, p. 7.

tions and dysfunctions of a very high order, perhaps of such a dimension that, if clearly exposed, they would challenge our very expectations of what a society is supposed to be.

Suppose, for instance, that our underlying conception of society (despite its flaws) is rational, purposeful, beneficent. Such a belief would explain why we are shocked by frequent instances of irrationality and malevolence, our own and others'. The rational expectation goes deep—into our anticipation of progress, ability to cure our ills, our assumption that in the end destiny is favorable. But imagine that the actuality is the opposite. *This* society is neither rational nor benevolent, but a real dog-eat-dog affair. Destiny or fate at best is neutral and perhaps negative in implications. Off on a mountain top on a vacation, we look back, and suddenly in the distance the America we have left behind seems bizarre and surreal. But suppose we are *not* tricked by distance and altitude, that what we have left behind is exactly what it seems to be from the mountain top: a mean-spirited society, a nation of Mafiamen, a pirate's den with piped music, a . . . a sort of "postindustrial" Byzantium, on slick paper, with unfairness, chicanery, and inequality built permanently into the social order. This is not a vision we should like to face, and as a practical matter of self-defense we would summon the distractions, fuzziness, illogic, and absurdities of the Fake Factor to shield our eyes from the pitiless stare of reality. The B.S. Factor would thus reassure us that our society is a normal and desirable place, that irrationality is rational, that sheer craziness is sane.

Or, imagine that the system, at bottom, is *mindless*. Those seemingly senseless routines that govern us—

the forms, the memos, the procedures—are not simply clumsy matters of organization which will eventually be improved, but necessary devices to fill up vast stretches of useless time and provide an excuse for meaningless effort. The widespread mediocrity is not a condition that will be replaced by excellence but a consummation to be wished. We would not want as a society to go beyond mediocrity because then the truth would be revealed: to fake it is to stand guard over emptiness.

Or, suppose the society is altogether *too* rational, to the point of being virtually out of human control. Society runs *us*, not we it. And that society *is* the machine, the technology, the sheer technique. This highly rationalized society automatically fits people into grooves and slots, selects them by remote control, places tremendous burdens and demands on them, patterns their destiny, and yields only the merest illusion of individual power. Such is the bleak vision of Jacques Ellul's *The Technological Society,* in which everything can be traced to the machine which progressively absorbs the individual. The anxiety aroused in him "by the turbulence of the machine is soothed by the consoling hum of a unified society." We do not like to think of ourselves as slaves. This vision is one we would attempt to avoid at all cost. The B.S. Factor would be used to insist that there is freedom and personal fulfillment when there is not.

It may be that all of these notions are true, or none of them. But before they are lightly discarded, observe that they provide a way to understand why the lie was superseded. It no longer sufficed for filling the need; it wasn't good enough, and the urgency for something workable was too great. The embracing self-deception of the B.S. Factor was, under the circumstances, a bet-

ter way. Now, it may be that our expectations are unreal, or that society is not performing as it should, or
both. It may be true that society would better spend its
energies making itself more coherent and less subject
to the contradictions from which the B.S. Factor arises.
The question is how to stop faking long enough to find
out what the real contradictions are.

V.

skeptics of the world, unite! or, the last real radicalism

ELP WANTED: a new kind of radical. I am sure many people are radical skeptics already, without having the vaguest idea they belong to the new wave. I doubt if they ever dreamed of being part of the van, of that phalanx of visionaries which always seems to arrive at the last critical moment, those Hairbreadth Harrys of History, to save the world just when it's slipping into the abyss. Nonetheless, something is clearly afoot, and they are part of it.

Afoot, in the air . . . exactly. This Radical Skepticism is in the air and people are into it. It's not something ready-made to slip into, like a suit off the rack, or join, like a church, or cheer for, like a hockey team. It's nothing you would ask the President to proclaim a Day for. It's not a philosophy or a Way. . . . It's an attitude, a point of view. People, millions on millions, have this underground *sense* that there must be an angle that cuts between the towers of trivia on the one side and the igloos of ideology on the other and gets somewhere—works! Only they can't decide exactly what it is. . . .

Of course, the fact that a radical skeptic decided she or he *was* a radical skeptic wouldn't mean he or she has to announce it. Some things you just don't talk about. Radical Skepticism sounds formal and pretentious—which is the last thing it is. Besides, the term is confusing. "Radical" sounds as if it meant radical about everything, which the radical *skeptic* is not. And "skeptic" sounds even worse. It was President Nixon himself who reminded us that *idealists,* not skeptics, build societies,* and who wants to be called a skeptic after that? Such a label: a tearer-down!

In any case, the radical skeptic is an idealist, though admittedly a rather odd-ball one. But far from being an ideological eccentric, he could enter an I-Am-an-American contest without qualms. Common sense, tough-mindedness, let's be happy . . . right on, as they say. In fact, Radical Skepticism *is* American. It wouldn't work anywhere else, in all probability, but we have the right traditions.

It may help dispel the armchair-critic idea of a skeptic if we ask what kind of protest movement the *radical* skeptics will mount when, before too long, they get together, perhaps even fielding a candidate for President. The radical skeptic would make an issue out of hypocrisy, systematic fakery, exaggeration, pretense . . . the B.S. Factor. It's a good issue and people will respond, only it needs to be dramatized. It needs a symbol —not an eagle or a donkey but a *garbage truck,* to make the connection between the garbage in the streets and

---

* See Chapter I.

in our minds. A slogan for the buttons and bumper stickers: "Eschew Obfuscation. Get Smart." The press could be challenged to present a daily Thought Pollution Index—not that it would, but at least reporters could be encouraged to attend the Platitude Recognition Training Sessions, the object being to raise cliché-consciousness and overcome the serious problem of cliché-deafness that settles over crowds and reporters alike when a speaker mounts to the podium. In these sessions, platitudes will be flashed on a screen, and if they are allowed to pass unchallenged the participants will receive electric shocks from wires attached to their skulls. Possible samples:

> The only solution to the Attica tragedy . . . [is a] genuine commitment of our vast resources to the human needs of all the people.
> —SENATOR EDMUND S. MUSKIE

> Organized religion—regardless of denomination—is an institution possessing a moral-ethical mandate.
> —SPIRO AGNEW

> But let me say one other thing. I think it is important that out of this mission we recognize that it was not a failure . . . The three astronauts did not reach the moon but they reached the hearts of millions of people in America and in the world. They reminded us in these days when we have this magnificent technocracy [sic] that men do count, the individual does count.
> —PRESIDENT NIXON

> We have learned from the students—from you and your contemporaries—that we must come up with better answers to larger questions.
> —SECRETARY OF TRANSPORTATION JOHN A. VOLPE

Audiences skilled in Platitude Recognition can deliver
a crushing blow—the mass yawn. This quickly forces
the speaker to take stock of himself.

A real though not insurmountable problem the radical skeptic faces is to communicate that the serious
and the whimsical are not deadly enemies. Many people have a sort of department-store view of the world:
a place for everything—The Serious Questions (nuclear
weapons, segregation, ecology) on one floor and the
stand-up comics on another. The radical skeptic, of
course, must not be confused with a Yippie! Politics, for
the radical skeptic, is not a matter of insulting the
police. (If he could, the radical skeptic would have the
police on his side.) It's just that the radical skeptic
takes humor seriously too.

On the substantive side of his program, the radical
skeptic seeks something different from the usual political goals. He is not, for one thing, an ideologist, and
he is also highly suspicious of words. He is forced,
therefore, to ask questions and to try to find accurate
gauges of performance as opposed to rhetoric. He might
suggest to politicians that politics is a profession and
should have professional standards, as law and medicine do. He might insist that a candidate he supports
take a sort of Hippocratic oath, for which I can find no
better terms than those suggested by Brendan Gill,
drama critic of *The New Yorker,* for playwrights to
follow. Readdressed to politicians, it would read:

> A politician purporting to relate facts must not
> tamper with the evidence; must not scramble
> reality and make-believe; must not introduce con-
> venient fictions for the sake of good dramatic effect
> or a so-called "higher" truth; must not take advan-

tage of the ignorance of his audience in order to
outwit them as a polemicist.

Come to think of it, not just politicians but everybody responsible for communications in any way ought
to take such a pledge. The point is, of course, to cut
through the thick grease and old varnish to discover
what kind of material lies beneath. And the best tool
the radical skeptic has is the *sharp* question—"Why?"
"What for?" "When?" "What do you mean?" "Who?"
These are terrifying questions, in a way, considering
how seldom they are answered. And when answers are
given, they don't appear to be the right answers.

1. Why are the people blamed for national failures?
The radical skeptic's impression is that a main source
of hypocrisy is the attempt to make responsibility collective. If *all* of us are blamed, the radical skeptic wonders, can *anyone* be blamed? But why charge an individual citizen with that over which he had no control?
(That he has so little power may not be his fault,
either.) The radical skeptic thinks that blame for failures should be isolated.

2. Is it fair to ask for something without giving something in return? In the name of unity or order, the citizen is asked to refrain from violence or pay a disproportionate share of the taxes without complaint. Is this
moral blackmail? Shouldn't there be a *quid pro quo* for
constructive participation? In exchange, shouldn't there
be a rather prompt solution to the slums, more fairly
distributed taxes, and so on? The radical skeptic thinks
that the citizen should indeed ask what his country does
for him.

3. When? To the radical skeptic, one of the chief

sources of hypocrisy is the failure to give delivery dates. Without a guarantee as to how much time will elapse before fulfillment, promises are just promises. Pledges for slum clearance or better schools should be accompanied by guarantees as to when such things will happen. *When* will the working hours be reduced? *When* do Americans get a month's paid vacation? When it comes to their future, more than they realize, Americans work in the dark.

4. What do you mean? The radical skeptic is generally wary of abstractions and wants words to be precise. A radical-skeptic platform writer, for instance, would never have titled the last three platforms of the Democrats "The Rights of Man," "One Nation, One People," "Toward a More Perfect Union." The radical skeptic distrusts abstractions like "man," "national interest," "progress," "dignity" because they can easily be masks for hiding meaning or generalizations for including those who might not want to be included.

5. Who has the power? Who is controlling what happens? Do those in authority deserve to be where they are? The radical skeptic, ever suspicious of nostrums, ever fearful that the eye does not focus on the real problems, ever wary of being led into cul-de-sacs, seeks always to find the real basis for things. Why, he asks, do so few have so much? And can vast wealth, often inherited, be separated from the uses of power?

This is only a sampling of the questions a radical skeptic would ask. The point is that such questions are designed to illuminate *what is happening* and they tend to take little for granted by way of conventional answers. The aim of the radical skeptic is to lower the confusion and eliminate the nonsense, hedges, and *non* *sequitur*s which make the American political dialogue something that approaches real *torture*.

Politics, however, isn't everything. In fact, the radical skeptic is not entirely, or even mainly, a political animal. He may easily have arrived at politics by the back door, as the only available way of doing things, but also as something to which he would not completely surrender himself. This radical skeptic could be a conservative, a liberal, a socialist, or a nothing (but not a know-nothing), just as he or she could be a doctor, lawyer, homemaker, factory worker. What makes him a radical skeptic is an attitude, and the way he arrived at it.

Let us now inquire more precisely what Radical Skepticism is and what stages of development the radical skeptic is likely to undergo. To be sure, there is no one route; there are no courses on the subject; there is no central meaning to be perceived such as that of the sound of one hand clapping. It is unlikely, though, that a radical skeptic ever simply emerges full-blown. Most probably, he arrived at his position as a result of experience, error, and disappointment, from which he emerged still in possession of his energies and purposes. If he had a starting point, it lay in his attitude toward "truth."

"Truth" was the prime mover in the first, or "detective," phase of his journey. Faced with endless contradictions in ideas, people, and things, he became impatient and frustrated. He set out on a quest to discover what was true and what false. If he could do it, he thought, he could find peace of mind in truth and certainty, and he considered all the arguments and doctrines with the idea of learning the right way or the true path. What he discovered, though, was that no serious truths are valid because for every good argument there was an equally good counterargument. A lot of people quit here and said, "That's horse racing." The fledgling radical skeptic didn't. He concluded only that, for him, nothing could be known for certain. This was his agnostic phase.

He pressed on. People knew him then by his habit of developing, and presenting skillfully, counterarguments for every argument. But soon he recognized that he was merely adding to the confusion, which is why he departed from the debater stage, though many do not. And, aware of the ease with which the other position could be developed, he began to lean toward suspending judgment altogether. In this period, you couldn't *make* him take a position. All possibilities seemed equally open (or closed), and no one system of values satisfied him. Words, especially, appeared to be very unreliable agents for defining reality—all they did was describe it, however poorly. This was when, in near despair, he almost succumbed to a condition of quietude and immobility. That was his neuter, or linguistic stage, where many lie buried.

However, the nagging contradictions that prompted him in his truth-trek back in the beginning still exist, and he knows it. His approach though, is different: now he can detach his own personality from the problem—that is, his own needs for whatever-it-is can be separated from his vision. But the real nature of things still seems as puzzling as the meaning of Outer Space, which makes him realize that his passivity was superficial and transitory. He begins to see the quest in a new light, because he has recognized a dilemma. On the one hand, the truth can't exist; on the other, he lives out his whole life acting as if some things were true, as when he walks across a floor without asking whether it will hold him. Of course, he tells himself, no truth is involved in the floor, merely confidence, which is a summing up of previous experience. But the question gets harder when beliefs are involved, because then, since he does think some things are more probable than others, he is forced to act as though some things were truer than others, even though nothing is finally true. But how does he establish the strength of the probability? Through reading the evidence, yes, but, in a more general sense, from what happens as a result of his own actions. This is different from the usual way of acting, it seems, because unlike those who proceed from an a priori idea that truth *does* exist, he himself can't *know* the truth. All he can do is experiment with things that seem sufficiently true.

At this point, he knows he must always act *as though* his assumptions were valid, without being really sure and always reserving the right to change his mind. He must act wholeheartedly, because only then can he give his assumptions a serious test by bringing his experiments to the point of actual results, which can be seen and measured. In trying to gauge the results he remains the questioner, the doubter, looking at the answers in as practical a way as he can, and as much as possible in terms of his everyday experience. He distrusts (though he doesn't necessarily reject) concepts and data. He tries to listen to his own *sense* of things, because he is part of the experiment. He hasn't abandoned his search for peace of mind, but he is moving in a new direction in his knowledge that he cannot establish the truth. Most of all, he does not want to be a skeptic, but no other road is open. He can't even be a

perfect skeptic, because there are too many "truths" he
secretly accepts without even knowing it. What he *can*
do is maintain his attitude of doubt while at the same
time trying to establish superior probabilities through
his actions. He takes as a sign of a healthy intelligence
the ability to keep contradictory arguments in mind
at the same time.

Doubt, for the radical skeptic, is a weapon. Note that
doubt is not the same as indecision and paralysis: it
makes him *act*. He does not act blindly—"Watch out,"
"Take your time," "Be careful," the radical skeptic tells
himself—but as his analysis leads him. He agrees with
Bertrand Russell that logic is the art of *not* drawing
conclusions; but his questions are frank, brutally frank,
and so are likely to be what conclusions he is able to
draw. He seeks to cut through, with his questions and
his sense of things, the propaganda and self-serving
syllogisms that dominate the mind of our time. He has
a feeling for limits and a desire to avoid futile controversy. His hatred of either/or reasoning, his dialectical
disposition to juxtapose contradictory arguments, help
him skirt the sham polemics and empty wars of position
that rage around him. His wariness of abstract logic
spares him from being stuck in time and mental space.
His avoidance of ideas based on fixed principles of mind
and human nature keeps him open to new experience.

He is now a radical skeptic, or the near approach:
skeptical because his habit of doubting, his suspicion
of "truth," goes to the grain; radical not only because
his skepticism calls for proof in action, but also because
his actions *are* experiments which he is willing to take
as far as the evidence lets him. Though he grasps the
contradictory nature of experiences, he does his best.
Dubious of conventional rationales, he is free to look

at the new. Because he is not tied to a set ideology, he can back off, admit mistakes, change his mind, try again. You will not, I think, normally find the radical skeptic among the suicides. For one thing, he has developed a good eye toward what he is responsible for and what is beyond his control, so that he is not nagged needlessly by self-pity, fear, and self-blame. For another, he is too curious about the results of his experiments, in terms of his personal growth and that of others. And, finally, he is too much of a believer in happiness.

The thrust of the radical skeptical position *is* happiness, his own and others'. Once you have cut away from the conceptualizations and the theories, happiness looms more and more as the supreme good and unhappiness as the ultimate evil. That simple message is what the radical skeptic has learned in his quest, and it was what causes him to ask always what aids human happiness. Does this? Does that? What's the payoff? Is there another way? Can what makes for unhappiness be avoided? Can what brings happiness be done?

Granted, there are rival claims on happiness, on justice, on survival, and the rest, but the present conceptual emphasis on the rivalries rather than the results of the rivalries prevents the deeper questions from being aired. And the fact that the radical skeptic would insist on airing them makes it unlikely that an elected government of radical skeptics would have fought the war in Vietnam. It would not have been so aimless and unquestioning in its vision as to permit, without a whimper, the American city to deteriorate, factionalism to degenerate almost to open class warfare, technology to become an end in itself, or rhetoric to have reached its present low estate. A government of radical skeptics would have tried to encourage just those uniquely American attributes which have been visibly and palpably neglected—the native American skepticism, love of happiness, fascination with experiments, practicality, hardheadedness, shrewdness, belief in common sense . . . the very attributes which (combined with national wealth enough to provide ample room for maneuver) might have produced perhaps an altogether new kind of society. And there is time. But first fakery . . . the Fake Factor . . . the B.S. Factor must be abolished, and only the radical skeptics can do the job. Skeptics, wherever you are, unite!

Some other books published by Penguin
are described on the following pages.

Jethro K. Lieberman

HOW THE GOVERNMENT BREAKS THE LAW

This startling book reveals that the greatest law-breaker in the United States is the government itself. The author aims to expose public officials who talk about "law and order," then twist, subvert, ignore, misunderstand, and thwart the law —and get away with it. Among much else, he discloses that authorities in Texas forced children into slavery, that prosecutors misrepresent evidence, that Congressmen lie, and that the Census Bureau cheats. Documented, nonpartisan, and clearheaded, *How the Government Breaks the Law* not only uncovers enough evidence to convict the guilty but also points the way toward sensible remedies. Jethro K. Lieberman has served as an adviser to two senators and to the President's Blue Ribbon Defense Panel.